THE WORLD'S GREATEST TOW TRUCKS
BY LOTUS PUBLICATIONS
PHOTOGRAPHY · EARL JOHNSON

THE WORLD'S GREATEST TOW TRUCKS©
PHOTOGRAPHY BY EARL JOHNSON
VOLUME III
DECEMBER 1995

This edition first published in 1996 by Motorbooks International Publishers & Wholesalers, 729 Prospect Avenue, PO Box 1, Osceola, WI 54020 USA

© EARL JOHNSON and Lotus Publications, 1995

Previously published by Lotus Publications, 1995

All rights reserved. With the exception of quoting brief passages for the purpose of review no part of this publication may be reproduced without prior written permission from the Publisher.

Motorbooks International is a certified trademark, registered with the United States Patent Office.

The information in this book is true and complete to the best of our knowledge. All recommendations are made without any guarantee on the part of the author or publisher, who also disclaim any liability incurred in connection with the use of this data or specific details.

We recognize that some words, model names and designations, for example, mentioned herein are the property of the trademark holder. We use them for identification purposes only. This is not an official publication.

Motorbooks International books are also available at discounts in bulk quantity for industrial or sales-promotional use. For details write to Special Sales Manager at the Publisher's address.

Library of Congress Cataloging-in-Publication Data Available.

ISBN 0-7603-0271-5

Printed in Hong Kong

PRODUCTION DESIGN BY HANNAH AKI HAWKINS

INTRODUCTION

In the making of any book there are many adventures, many unexpected bends in the road and many challenges. This book is no different. It would never be possible without the people whose equipment is shown on these pages, people whose work often goes unrewarded and unnoticed. The quality of the equipment in this book exceeds minimum standards because the owners themselves exceed minimum standards. They would be standouts in any field they chose. So we begin by thanking them for the participation and for the pride they have in the difficult service they offer 24 hours a day, 365 days a year.

Earl Johnson traveled overland more than 20,000 miles to photograph all the trucks in this book. Over a period of 9 months, including 4,000 more miles in Europe, the weather held out -- for the most part -- astonishingly well, and busy companies pulled their fleet's flagship truck out of service for a few hours for the photo session. During one 90 day period, Earl was never home once. The result is a cross section of the industry with an expanded European section that will be interesting to many for years to come.

Dedicated to John L. Hawkins, II

One regret remains. In April 1995 the person whose long shadow falls over so much that has been accomplished in the towing and recovery industry died in Chattanooga, Tennessee. Thirteen years earlier, John Hawkins and Earl Johnson (over a sundown bottle of scotch at one of the first tow shows in Lake George, New York) talked about such a book. He knew this volume was underway but never saw it completed. Thanks are due nevertheless, to a visionary who never stopped helping things happen.

A list of people who should receive special notice would be a long one, since it starts with all the people in the book. We specially

Grace Hawkins and Earl Johnson

want to mention our staff, Stacey Quinn, Gail Goretsky and Hannah Hawkins. While we were in Europe, we had extraordinary hospitality and assistance from Michael Boniface at Boniface Engineering in Thetford, England. Mike opened the doors to his office for us for several days. Failing that, we never could have contacted busy owners, reserved time, and shot 28 trucks in under 21 days. In the same way Mike helped us defeat the British phone system, Jean Jacques Julien of Dépann 2000 in Paris helped us conquer the unfamiliar French phones. He spent the better part of 4 days assisting us, and for the owner of what is perhaps the world's largest operation in a city wracked at the time by terrorist bomb threats, that was no small matter. We are very grateful as well as amazed. He says, "it's normal!"

Merci, Jean-Jacques!

Others who stand out in directing us to the world's greatest tow trucks are Jean Georges of Jigé Lohr in Révigny, France, Patrick Vasseur of CEV in Ecquevilly, France, my brother John Hawkins of Miller Industries and Don "Your Favorite Texan" Walters of DeWalt in Houston. We regret missing some equipment we knew to be well qualified due to the constraints of time and distance, but a future volume will offer the opportunity to include more of the trucks large and small we did not shoot this time.

A last word to the casual reader of this book. When you look out on any street or highway, remember that it is passable because of the towing and recovery industry. Without the hard working men and women who respond under often difficult and even tragic circumstances at any time to a phone call for help, transport everywhere would grind to a miserable halt. Enjoy the beautiful tow trucks in these pages, from the snappiest light duty tow truck to the most overwhelming heavy duty recovery unit. They are brought to you by their owners, always at your service!

In Chattanooga, Tennessee, the International Towing and Recovery Hall of Fame and Museum opened in 1995. It is an entertaining and educational must-see for anyone interested in antique trucks and a lasting memorial to the many who have worked tirelessly in the field. It would never have existed without the dogged determination of the person to whom this book is dedicated, John L. Hawkins, II. We encourage everyone to visit this building and browse through the constantly changing exhibits. You'll find this book on sale there as a fund-raiser, and we'd like to thank the Museum for including it in its displays.

Grace M. Hawkins

FRONT AND BACK COVER SPECIFICATIONS

Ernie's of Vernon Hills, Illinois

Ernie and Julie Vole started Ernie's Wrecker Service in June of 1956. In the beginning the fleet consisted of one truck which Ernie Vole had built himself! Over the last forty years the fleet has grown to 25 trucks and various pieces of equipment, while the personnel has grown to 30, including staff for a full service garage and fuel pumps. The Voles have 4 sons and 1 daughter, all of whom are involved in the business.

This 1991 Oshkosh 4 axle 6 wheel drive has a Cummins Big Cam IV engine, 18 speed transmission and airbrakes. The GVW is a hefty 91,000 lbs, the wheelbase is 320" and the truck is 39' long. It has a 25,000 lb. front axle, a 65,000 lb. rear axle and a 25,000 lb. airlift axle. The towing equipment is by Bill Bottoms. The 70 ton Rotator model has a 3 stage hydraulic boom with 140,000 lbs. capacity. There are two 35,000 lb. DP planetary winches and one 15 ton Ramsey holding winch. The truck also features 2-way radio, siren, emergency strobe light and telephone. Over the past 5 years this truck has been used hundreds of times for major truck accidents and is responsible for saving four lives over those years.

World Class of Auburn, Pennsylvania

World Class Automotive is based in Auburn, Pennsylvania, in the beautiful rolling hills near Reading. A full service operation in business at their present location since 1985, World Class started with one truck in a neighboring state in 1980 and now has a diverse fleet of 11 trucks on the road, and 10 full time plus 4 part time employees. In addition to the towing operation, which includes underwater recoveries, Jan and Ron Weick specialize in Jeep Wranglers. They buy, sell, convert and handle all accessories for these as well as other vehicles. World Class has a dealer license, full service repair facility and also buys and sells used parts.

This stunning light duty tow truck glows with 134 marker lights plus fog lights for safety and a ground effect kit for style. It's a Dodge Ram 3500 4 x 4 with a V8 Magnum 5.2 liter engine, 5 speed transmission, hydraulic brakes, 139" wheelbase and an 11,000 lb. GVW. The truck's NoMar hydraulic wheelift is equipped with a 4 ton hydraulic boom, a single cable 8,000 lb. capacity winch, and the unit also sports an XS strobe bar atop the cab.

INDEX BY NAME

Page		Page		Page		Page		Page	
115	A & M Automotive Tim Nall 1212 Elon Place High Point, NC 27263 910/889-6000 Fax 919/883-4862	16	Battleground Wrecker Service Steve Bowman 6204 S. NC 62 Burlington, NC 27215 800/672-3122 Fax 910/227-6998	24	Chuck's Towing Service Chuck Mason 48 W. Taylor Avenue Hamilton, NJ 08610 609-888-4020	33	Dépannage Medici Rolland Medici Rue de Paris S'Quen L'Aumone, France 95310 1 34 64 3 24	40	Excalibur Towing Service Corp. Ramon Crego 14294 S.W. 142nd Avenue Miami, FL 33186 305/235-6065 Fax 305/378-4527
9	Al Valk's Garage Al Valk 2359 Albany Post Road Walden, NY 12586 914/778-3698	17	Beaty's Wrecker Service Perry Beaty 2426 Berryhill Road Charlotte, NC 28208 704-338-9360 Fax 704/342-4135	25	Clarence Cornish Wrecker Svc George Escott 2557 S. Riverside Drive Ft. Worth, TX 76104 817/535-6565 Fax 817/535-6555	34	DeWalt Manufacturing Don Walters 15653 North Brentwood Channelview, TX 77530 713/452-1081 Fax 713/452-3325	41	Exclusive Towing Jerry Kohutek 3777 Placentia Lane Riverside, CA 92501 909-682-2003
10	Arcade Motors. Ltd. David Brinklow 198 Great Cambridge Road Enfield, Middlesex UK EN1 1UG	18	Berry Brothers Bob Berry 598 55th Street Oakland, CA 94609 510/465-7215 Fax 510-653-3263	26	Classic Towing Bobby Reynolds 1234 Route 17K Montgomery, NY 12549 914/427-9920	35	Douglas Karlsson A.B. Hakan Karlsson Urstegen 5 Skøvde, Sweden 54145 46/0500 48 69 00	42	Falzone's Towing Paul Falzone 365 Pierce Street Kingston, PA 18704 717/823-2100 Fax 717/288-7487
11	Ashland Towing Mike Early PO Box 715 Ashland, OR 97520 503/482-8770	19	Bill & Wags Towing Bill Robertson 1516 S. Bonview Avenue Ontario, CA 91761-4407 909/923-6100 Fax 909/923-6108	27	Coleman Motor Company Cary Coleman 30 Briscoe Lane Fredericksburg, VA 22401 703/898-4295 Fax 703/786-2431	36	Drake Towing Ltd. Tom English 1553 Powell Vancouver, B.C. V5L 1H2 604/251-3344 Fax 604/251-6206	43	Farrington Truck Parts Dewey Farrington 1001 S.W. 3rd Street Oklahoma City, OK 73126 405/239-7586 Fax 405/239-7908
12	Ashman's Auto Body Michael Ashman P.O. Box 6 Washington, NJ 07882 908-689-1662 Fax 908/689-0665	20	Bob Bolin Services Bob Bolin #5 Industrial Lane Florissant, MO 63031 314/831-8800 Fax 314/831-5141	28	Costigan's Bill Costigan 42 Derwood Circle Rockville, MD 20850 301/251-1400 Fax 301/251-2675	37	Driscoll's Towing Bob & Marian Driscoll 1701 N Dixie Hwy Pompano Beach, FL 33060 305/946-4747 Fax 305/781-0056	44	Fillongley Garage Eric Hammond Tamworth Road, Fillongley S. Yorkshire, UK CV7 8DY 01676 540267 Fax 01676 542 867
13	Auto Recovery & Repair Graham Kidger Woodhouse Mill Service Station A57 Retford Road Sheffield, S. Yorkshire UK S13 9WF 01142 691 010 Fax 01142 691 581	21	Buckdale Garage John & Jill Huckle Elstow Storage Depot Kempston Hardwick, UK 01234-740 698 Fax 01234-742 501	29	D & G Cars Mick Jennings Units D1-D3, Sterling Industrial Estate, Rainham Road, S. Dagenham, Essex, UK RM10 8TX 0181 984 7247 Fax 0181 593 5671	38	DuBois Towing Dick and Fay Boggs 500 S. Atchison St. Anaheim, CA 92805 714/772-9510 Fax 714/772-3274	45	Fox Towing Bob Baker 8741 North Gilmore Road Fairfield, OH 45014 513/874-4271 Fax 513/874-0404
14	Autos Polyservices Remorquage Dominique Antonmattei 65 Ave Faidherbe 93100 Montreuil FRANCE 1 48 58 08 90	22	C & L Charlie Napoli, Jr. 73 Eagle Rock Ave East Hanover, NJ 07936 201/386-9866 Fax 201/386-1870	30	Dave's Towing Dave Barton P.O. Box 1305 Stockton, CA 95201 209/951-9251 Fax 209/462-8009	39	Eagle Automotive Bob Newell 261 Parsippany Road Parsippany, NJ 07054 201/884-2742	46	Fred's Automotive Fred Viohl 7 Samsondale Avenue Haverstraw, NY 10907 914/429-3894 Fax 914/429-3911
15	Bakker Service Station George Bakker 4640 Furman Avenue New York, NY 10470 718/324-1223 Fax 718/324-1350	23	Central Service Tim West 1113 Central Avenue Albany, NY 12205 518/459-8549 Fax 518/459-4771	31	Dépann 2000 Jean-Jacques Julien 142-144 av du Maréchal deLatte de Tassigny Les Lilas FRANCE 93260 43 62 2000 Fax 43 62 2002	cover	Ernie's Towing Ernie Vole 909 S. Milwaukee Avenue Vernon Hills, IL 60061 708/634-3737 Fax 708/634-8142	47	Garner's Family Enterprises, Inc. Jamey Garner 410 East Broadway Fortville, IN 46040 317/485-5506 Fax 317/485-4867

Page		Page		Page		Page		Page	
48	Gate City Towing Bill Washam 4513 Drummond Road Greensboro, NC 27320 910/292-1422 Fax 910/292-1464	118	J & J Towing Joe Leapby 5463 Southern Maryland Blvd Lothian, MD 20711 800/832-8978	61	Lancaster's Garage Larry Lancaster 191 Troxler Circle Concord, NC 28027 704/786-5144 Fax 704/782-7165	69	Moorman's Randy and Sue Arnett 419 S. Miami Avenue Xenia, OH 45385 513/372-9666 Fax 513/372-2072	77	Patriot Towing Arlan White 3753 Placentia Lane Riverside, CA 92501 909/787-0393 Fax 909/787-0202
00	Gene's Towing Michael Myers 9212 S. Tacoma Way Tacoma, WA 98499 206/588-1757 Fax 206/582-8816	54	J & K Recovery, Ltd. Kevin McFadden Grovebury Road Leighton Buzzard, Beds, UK LU7 8SQ 01525-255-4041 Fax 01525-850-361	62	Lewis Wrecker Service Terry Lewis 1301 22nd Ave Heights Meridien, MS 39301 601/693-0225 Fax 601/693-0245	70	Nadler Garage Jean Michel et Joelle Nadler 583 Impasse des Romains 51700 Les Mesnils FRANCE 83 81 14 04	78	Petroff Towing Ed Petroff 3801 N. 89th Street Caseyville, IL 62232 618/398-6000 Fax 618/398-6136
49	Great America Towing Dino Tomassi 560 Gish Road Santa Clara, CA 95112 408-283-8571 Fax 408/287-3184	55	Jack's Bill and Claudia Shuttleworth 2075 Paramount Abbotsford B.C. V2S 4N5 604/864-0066 Fax 604/853-6645	63	Lisi's Towing Anthony Lisi RT. 6 Brewster, NY 10509 914-278-6166	71	Negoshian Enterprises Ed Negoshian 14 Elliott Street Newton, MA 02161-1605 617/965-9999 Fax 617/527-6704	79	Phil's Towing Phil Esposito 1716 South 25th Street Philadelphia, PA 19145 215/365-0106 Fax 215/334-5059
50	Harveys Recovery Harvey Wasson 34 Edward Tyler Road Coventry, W. Midlands UK CV7 9PF 01203 318054 Fax 01203 314 741	56	Jack's Wrecker Service Larry L. Jones P.O. Box 16 Pickerington OH 43147 614/800/307-8697	64	M&W Towing Mark Sussino 811 Route 46 East Parsippany, NJ 07054 201/263-2131 Fax 201/402-2622	72	New York Recovery Don Cherico 126 Lafayette Avenue N. White Plains, NY 10603 914/949 -7889 Fax 914/949-3298	80	R. Mayer of Atlanta Ronnie Mayer 3302 Hardee Avenue Chamblee, GA 30041 404/457-6246 Fax 404/455-7259
51	Hendrickson Towing Tommy Probst 1026 E. Jericho Tpke. Huntington Station, NY 11746 516/423-6616 Fax 516/424-0047	57	Jenkins Wrecker Service Kenneth and Regina Jenkins 6937 Chapman Road Lithonia, GA 30058 404/482-8373 Fax 404/482-9530	65	McAllisters Recovery Frank McAllister Hollybush Ind. Park, Hollybush Lane Aldershot, Hants UK 01252 229 09 Fax 01252 345 435	73	Nowell's Towing Steve Nowell 15704 Jeff Davis Hwy Woodbridge, VA 22191 703/670-0400 Fax 703/878-6996	81	R.U.D. Commercials Bob Hunt Corngreaves Ind. Estate, Chilerton Rd Cradley Heath, W. Midlands UK 01384 562 222 Fax 01384 412 435
52	Hugh's Body Shop & Truck Svc Hugh Simmons 2255 Lee Highway N Troutville, VA 24175 703/992-2543 Fax 703/992-2523	58	Kenfield Motor Recovery, Ltd. Colin Jeffries Unit 13, Chesterfield Way, Pump Lane Hayes, Middlesex UK UB3 3NW 0181-569-2323 Fax 0181 569 3710	66	McCarty & Sons Towing & Lowbed Service Bill McCarty 1608 E. 5th Street Oxnard, CA 93031 805/487-0117 Fax 805/486-3213	74	Official Towing, Inc. Marty Lewicki 19801 Pleasant St. Clair Shores MI 48080 1-800-777-6840 Fax 810/771-5869	82	Ramont's Tow Service Barry Vallerand 1106 N. 9th Modesto CA 95350 209/527-2700 Fax 209/527-0567
53	Interstate Chaparral Towing Junior Vandervort P.O. Box 15183 Austin, TX 78761 512/835-6580 Fax 512/990-1681	59	Lakeside Towing James Fernhoff P.O. Box 10 Truckee, CA 96162 916/587-6000 Fax 916/587-5114	67	McKinney Wrecker Service Gene McKinney Rt. 2 Box 2 West Blocton, AL 35184 205/938-7705	75	Paddack's Wrecker Service, Inc. Jeff Ripley 18702 U.S. 31 North Westfield, IN 46074 317/896-3206 Fax 317/867-0651	83	Randy's Towing Randy Houston 2135 Elmway Okanagan, WA 98840 800/553-4466 Fax 509/422-2322
117	J & J Towing Joe Cammarata 5613 N. W. 8th Street Margate, FL 33063 305/972-0855 800/972-0855 Fax 305/972-7383	60	Lamb & Mansfield Darrell Mansfield Unit 1, Harpur Hill Industrial Est. Buxton, Derbyshire UK SK17 9JL 01298 72399 Fax 01298 73046	68	Milford Towing & Service Don and Sue Trammell 785 St. Rte 50 Milford, OH 45150 513/831-0924 Fax 513/576-8441	76	Palace Garage Bill Hemenez 1609 Abram Court San Leandro, CA 94577 510/483-8200 Fax 510/483-1748	84	Rangeline Towing Max Bobko 8000 W. Atlantic Ave. Delray Beach, FL 33446 407/499-1879 Fax 407/495-8051

Page		Page		Page		Page		Page	
85	Reed's Inc Dan Reed 1030 3rd Street N.W. Massillon, OH 44647 216/833-2823 Fax 216/833-0392	93	Schlager Auto Body Repair, Inc. Jimmy Schlager P.O. Box 470 Milton, MA 02186 617/282-1120 Fax 617/282-0788	100	Superior Towing Pat Kirk 1869 Service Court Riverside, CA 92507 909/845-6457 Fax 909/682-1261	107	Wards Of Burnley Graham Ward Lane End Garage, Burnley Lancaster UK BB12 6LN 01282 34923	113	WreckMaster Donnie Cruse P.O. Box 473 Lewiston, NY 14092 800/267-2266 Fax 905/643-6129
86	Reynolds Towing Greg Reynolds 210 E. University Champaign, IL 61820 800/242-8694 Fax 217/352-9277	94	Schmitz Service, Inc. Eric Schmitz 8526 Leesburg Pike Vienna, VA 22182 703/827-0611 Fax 703/827-2645	101	Technique Towing Kevin Rodgerson 2495 N. Miami Fresno, CA 93727 209/291-9813 Fax 209/291-3237	108	Watty Garage bvba Robert Watty Brugsesteenweg 73 Oudenburg, Belgium 8460 01032 059 26 87 78 Fax 01032 059 26 81 62		
87	Rose Ledge Companies Tim Tierney P.O. Box 64 Millers Falls, MA 01349-0064 413/659-3563 Fax 413/659-3188	119	Select Towing Svc. John McElroy P.O. Box 637 West Orange, NJ 07051 201/325-7898 Fax 201/325-0138	102	Ted's Of Fayville Peter Aspesi 5 Park Street Southborough, MA 01772 508/485-0503 Fax 508/481-6290	109	Weber's Truck Service Kenny Weber 520 Capitol Drive Pewaukee, WI 54072 414/691-0333 Fax 414/691-7472		
88	S & H Recovery Services Ltd James & John Sparrow Redhouse Garage, Gt North Road Woodlands, Doncaster, S. Yorks, UK 01302 724 454 Fax 01302-727-038	95	Shaw Brothers Stephen Shaw 129 London Rd, Markyate St. Albans, Herts UK AL3 8JR 01 582 842 432 Fax 01 582 841 764	103	Transport Towing Bill Parks 2615 Brandon Road Joliet, IL 60436 800/292-5072 Fax 815/727-1360	110	Williams Truck & Equipment Svc. Johnny Williams Rte 3, Box 20 Williams Rd Bay City, TX 77414 409/245-4992 call Fax 409/245-1288		
89	S.A. Braun Louis Braun 4, rue de Paris, "La Croix Charon" Le Mesnil Amelot, France 77990 1-60 03 24 24 Fax 1-60 03 16 39	96	Shroyer's & Central Towing Inc. Daniel Shroyer 613 Poxson Lansing, MI 48910 517/487-2400 Fax 517/487-5645	104	Truck Tires, Inc/Overland Equipment Jim Mills 3900 A White Tire Rd. Landover, MD 20785 800-386-3232 Fax 301/773-2594	111	Wilton Service Center Tom Luciano 215 Ballard Road Gansevoort, NY 12831 (518)584-1444		
90	Sam's Towing Eddie Hornbostel 9500 Franklin Avenue Franklin Park, IL 60131 708/455-2610 Fax 708/455-4521	97	Skeet's Roy Hartis 303 4th Street SE Conover, NC 28613 704/464-9162	105	Tumino Towing John Tumino 219 Fort Lee Rd Teaneck, NJ 07666 201/947-7600 Fax 201/836-3705	112	Winebrenner's Auto & Truck Svcs Clinton Winebrenner 222 South Abbe Road Elyria, OH 44035 216/322-5419		
91	Sandy's Towing Ted Durig 139 Auto Club Drive Dayton, OH 45459 513/461-4980 Fax 513/294-6980	98	SOS Recovery Trevor Roper Recovery Hse, Marsh Grove, Thornton Lane Bradford UK BD5 9EN 01274 735 299 Fax 01274 521 827	106	Upman's Randy and Lisa Upman 3107 Clarke Road Sarasota, FL 34231 813/924-7084 Fax 813/921-7980	114	Woody's Wrecker Service Woody Page 1601 East Taylor Waco, TX 76705 817/752-0535 Fax 817/867-8335		
92	Santa Fe Tow Service Jon Kupchin 9930 Lackman Lenexa, KS 66219 800/927-5201 Fax 913/894-2550	99	Statewide Towing & Recovery Chris Kirk 190 N. Main Street Riverside, CA 92519 909/682-9336 Fax 909/682-3529	120	Van Amerongen b.v. Hendrick Van Amerongen Boulevard Heuvelink 2B-4 6828 KP Arnhem Holland 85 51 52 53 Fax 85 42 06 40	back cover	World Class Automotive Ron White R.D. #2 Box 64B Auburn, PA 17922 717/366-1900 Fax 717/366-1007		

Al Valk's Garage in Walden, New York was started in 1950 by Al Valk, Sr. In 1969 Al Jr. took over and the business grew into the largest independent repair facility in Orange County with a ten bay garage, three heavy duty wreckers, three flatbeds, two light duty wreckers, two road service vans and an antique wrecker. The shop runs a 24 hour emergency towing and truck road service that services one of the busiest crossroads in America where I-84 meets I-87.

The truck shown here is a 1982 Mack Cruiseliner Cabover with a 6 cylinder 300 Maxidyne engine. The wheelbase stretches 260". It has a 5 speed transmission and a GVW of 44,000 lbs. The towing equipment is a DeWalt 3540 with a hydraulic extension boom and two 45,000 lb. twin winches. It features GE 2-way radio and GE N.Y.S. Thruway radio.

Boniface have been engineering recovery equipment at their factory in Thetford, Norfolk, England since 1982 and have established themselves as one of the largest manufacturers of heavy duty equipment with a reputation for quality and innovation. The example shown here is from their Recoverer range which features an underreach with an extension of 156" and a two-stage boom which provides 20 tonne (44,000 lbs.) lifting capacity when extended. This specification can only be achieved by using the grades of steel and manufacturing techniques which have just become available in the 90's.

Boniface's product range includes the Interstater, or Masterlift as it is known in Germany, which is a recovery unit widely used across the world. The Renault Magnum illustrated was built for Arcade Motors of Enfield, North London, and is regarded as being the first recovery unit based on this chassis in use in the UK. The photograph was taken only after Earl Johnson convinced Michael Boniface to drive into a field shortly after it had been harvested, without the permission of the farmer to whom the field belonged! While Michael shuffled nervously from foot to foot, the intrepid photographer snapped enthusiastically, muttering publishing-type comments like "that'll copy" and "great shot." Fortunately the shoot was completed uninterrupted.

Ashland Towing was started in 1979, and has been a family owned business since 1981. The truck shown here is a Peterbilt 379 with a 475 Detroit engine. The wheelbase is 300" and the GVW is 58,860 lbs. It has a 13 speed transmission and a 2 speed Eaton 54,000 lb. rear end. The Century 1040 boom is a 3 stage hydraulic with 45 ton capacity and 2 speed 40 ton winches. The truck also features a Motorola Syntorex 9000 radio system.

Ashman's Auto was started in 1974 and serves the area of Washington, New Jersey. The 1995 International 4700 shown here has a Turbo diesel engine with 200 HP, an Allison automatic transmission and Power Disc 4 wheel brakes. Its GVW is 24,500 lbs. and its wheelbase is 192". The towing equipment is an AATAC 19' aluminum bed with independent wheelift which has a remote free spool winch with cable tension. The truck also features 2-way radio, CB, custom exhaust, AM/FM stereo disc player and Alcoa aluminum wheels. The GMC HD3500 1992 truck on the right, model TC31403, has a 454 CI V-8 engine and a HD 4 speed automatic transmission.   Its wheelbase is 160", GVW is 15,000 lbs. and it has Power Disc 4 wheel brakes. The towing equipment is a Vulcan 804 UBXL with a 4 ton hydraulic wheelift and single cable winch.   This truck features 2-way radio, CB, AM/FM stereo cassette, custom side exhaust, oak interior with custom seats, 200 extra lights and Alcoa aluminum wheels.

APR est une entreprise dynamique dirigée de main de maitre par M. et Mme. Dominique. La société possède une trentaine de véhicules que tout le monde connait dans la région parisienne grace à ses couleurs specifiques jaune et verte ainsi que l'entretien et un état de présentation irreprochable, le tout associé à des camions et à des équipments haut de gamme. qui procurent un service de très haut niveau à la clientèle. Ici ils présentent un Mercedes 1217 cabine passager 6 places empattement 42. Equipement Jigé Lohr simplex basculant coulissant force 4T avec panier Flèche AR. Jupe polyester latérale. Treuil hydraulique 4T commande radio. Le Toyota PPZJ 75 PTC 3Ts 4x4, moteur 6 cyl diesel 130 HP, suspension renforcé par coussin d'air. Equipement Mid City Jigé Lohr, capacité bras allongé 1200 kg, bras retracté 1700 kg. Correction d'assiette 15 °, extension du bras, 300 m/m

APR is a dynamic company operated by the husband and wife team Dominique. Known all over Paris for its outstanding green and yellow color scheme as well as the cleanliness of all vehicles, APR delivers an unusually high level of service with thirty-some trucks to its many clients. Here you see one of their Mercedes, a model 1217 with a 6 passenger compartment. The slideback is by Jigé Lohr, with a radio-controlled winch, polyester side skirt and a 2 ton grid and crane combination. The Toyota model PPZJ 75 GVW 3Ts 4x4, 6 cyl diesel 130 HP has air reinforced rear suspension. The towing equipment is a Jigé Lohr Mid City with an extended stinger lifting capacity of 1200 kilos, retracted stinger capacity 1700 kgs. The hydraulic tilt down angle is 15° and the stinger stroke is 300 mm.

Auto Recovery Services, the company known throughout the United Kingdom for its well-maintained equipment and courteous staff, opened for business in 1979 under the leadership of the present managing director and owner Graham Kidger. The staff of 35 now handles the needs of Auto Recovery's many clients with a fleet of 25 vehicles. Graham Kidger was inducted into the International Towing and Recovery Hall Of Fame in 1992.

The sleeper cab Scania 8 x 2 shown here is a Model 142 V8 with a 480 Scania engine. Overall wheelbase is 5,530 mm and GVW is 22 tons. The Boniface Interstater is a MK IIE 25 ton capacity unit equipped with 2 Superwinch H30s. The Ford/Iveco shown here is a Eurocargo E75.15 with a 150 Turbo engine. The Whitacres crew cab with a GVW of 7,500 lbs. sports a slide back car carrier and second car lift mechanism manufactured by Dyson/Brimec Recovery Systems and served by a DP winch. Two-way and mobile radios keep these two beauties in contact with their home base in Sheffield, England.

For over 70 years Bakker Service has been specializing in commercial vehicle maintenance, recovery and transportation. These two trucks are part of the Bakker service team that services the greater metropolitan New York area. The service truck on the left has a V-8 diesel engine with an Allison automatic transmission, AC/DC welder, torch set-up, fuel transfer pump set-up and an 8,000 watt generator. The unit carries nylon, water and hi-pressure hoses with fittings and a complete set of tools.

The heavy duty truck on the right has a set back front, 20,000 lb. axle, lo-hole transmission, air ride pusher lift axle and rear axle. It also has an RB Mack extra capacity double frame. The body is custom BAKKER fabricated featuring modular left and right slide off assemblies with modular rear stiff legs manufactured by BAKKER. Each leg has a 15 ton capacity. The Trebron under-lift was installed by BAKKER. The unit can be controlled from inside the cab or remotely.

Battleground Wrecker Service was started in 1970 by the Bowman family. The front truck shown here is a 1989 Peterbilt model 377 with an NTC 400 Cummins engine. It has a 9 speed Fuller transmission and features a Jake brake and heated mirrors. The towing equipment is a 50 ton DeWalt with two 30,000 lb. DP winches and a 35,000 lb. underreach boom.

The rear truck is a 1984 Peterbilt model 359 with an NTC 350 Cummins engine. It has a 15 speed Fuller transmission with a Jake brake, heated mirrors and a walk-in sleeper. The towing equipment is an Atlas 40 ton with an add-on Ray-lift underreach. It features two 25,000 lb. Ramsey winches. Both trucks feature 2-way radios and cellular phones.

Beaty's Wrecker Service has been serving the metro Charlotte, North Carolina area for nearly forty years. This 1988 Peterbilt with a 350 Cummins engine has a 9 speed transmission on a 372" wheelbase. The GVW is 38,000 lbs. It features Reyco suspension with trailer overload that enables it to tow a loaded semi.

The Holmes 750 towing equipment with Grant 50 plus hydraulic conversion has a Z-20 Zacklift. The boom has a 100,000 lb. capacity fully extended with a 26' hook height. It features 25,000 lb. Holmes mechanical dual winches. This handsome truck is driven by Jeff Keziah.

Berry Brothers Towing was started in 1973. The truck shown here is a 1995 Freightliner model FLD 120 Classic with a Caterpillar 3406E 435 HP engine. The wheelbase is 298". It has a Roadranger 18 speed transmission with a GVW of 60,600 lbs. The front axle is 14,600 lbs. and the rear axle is 46,000 lbs. The brakes are Rockwell. It features air conditioning, power steering, cruise control, leather seats, air ride suspension and air ride cab. The towing equipment is a Challenger model CH30. It has an integrated boom and underreach (35,000 lbs.) with a capacity of 30 tons and two 30,000 lb. DP winches. Special features include on board scales and "Power Up" controls. Operated by Bob Berry, this company serves the Oakland-San Francisco area and was among the first to respond after the devastating 1989 earthquake which leveled sections of the nearby freeway. Bob is a member of the Towing and Recovery International Hall Of Fame and a recipient of many awards for service to his state and neighbors.

Bill & Wag's first opened for business in Ontario, California in 1963. Headquartered in one of the United States' most heavily populated and traveled areas, Bill & Wag's has built a loyal and satisfied customer base by offering top quality service by friendly people with their customers always first in mind. This 1987 Kenworth K-100 has a Cummins 400 engine on a 287" wheelbase with a 12" setback. It has a 13 speed 14613 transmission. The truck, which has a GVW of 50,000 lbs. and S-Cam brakes, has DS 380 rears and an eight bag air ride. It also has Jake brakes, Alcoa wheels, wheelift attachment and tow-bar extension. The towing equipment is a BRO model 202 with a 55,000 lbs. capacity and a 75,000 lb. main winch with a 22,000 lb. auxiliary. It features a 2-way radio, back-up monitor, air-weigh scales and a 60" sleeper. This truck is driven and cared for by Harold "Jay" Strawderman.

Bill Robertson and his staff cordially invite you to visit Bill & Wags if you are visiting in the Los Angeles area.

Bob Bolin Services has been in business for more than forty years. Operating out of St. Louis, they offer everything from wreckers and rollbacks to equipment hauling. Founder Bob Bolin has been the pillar of the company, and now has turned over general operations of the company to son Mike. The flatbed operation is run by son Greg, and Bob's daughter Nancy Cotner is the invaluable administrative manager.

The 1992 Peterbilt 377 pictured here is just one of the many impressive trucks at Bob Bolin Services. It has a Caterpillar 3406 350 HP engine and a 298" wheelbase. The 9 speed Fuller transmission has carried this truck through many rescue missions. The towing equipment is a Century 5030/T with wheelift attachments. It features a 2-way radio, CB, TV and sleeper.

Buckdale Recovery are situated in Kempston Hardwick, Bedfordshire, England between the A1 and M1. The company is well known for its innovative designs and this Scania 8 x 4 is no exception. Presenting a clean and distinctive image to the motoring public as well as to its commercial clientele, the equipment was built to John Huckle's specification using components from British Interstater, Swedish BRO and Danish Nielson manufacturers. The tail plane rear flyer incorporates a pendulum system allowing the rear beacons to remain horizontal when the crane is lifted. A long reach Hiab knuckleboom crane 950 is fitted and a fold-up framework allows wrecked vehicles to be carried above the underlift. The Scania has a UK plated weight of 31,800 kgs distributed as follows: 6,500 kgs on each front axle and 9,400 kgs on the rear. Gross train weight is 78,000 kgs.

C **& L** is a full service towing operation located in East Hanover, New Jersey. Owned by Charlie Napoli, Jr., C & L presents this 1990 Kenworth T600 3406B single axle with a 13 speed transmission. The working end of the truck is a Challenger 35 ton boom with underlift and includes an air pusher axle.

Serving Albany, the capitol city of New York, for the past ten years, **Central Service Center,** owned by Timothy J. West, presents this International 4700 series. This truck with an Allison automatic transmission, DT 366 engine and custom designed subframe for lower loading angle was specially manufactured for the extremely high volume of work Central Service performs for its customers. The specially designed headache-rack enables easy loading of limousines. In addition, an independent 3,000 lb. capacity wheelift allows multi-vehicle transporting. The 1-800-2BE-TOWED number took months of research but has paid off in name recognition and ease of recall all over the area.

Chuck's Towing Service was started in 1985 by Chuck Mason. This photo was taken in early 1995, and is the latest of many photos the photographer Earl Johnson has taken of Chuck's trucks. The truck shown here is a 1994 Western Star model 4969 F. It has a 3406 Caterpillar 350 HP engine with a Jake brake. Its wheelbase is 269" and it has a 15 speed Fuller transmission with a GVW of 35,000 lbs. It features an AM/FM cassette stereo, deluxe interior and air conditioning.

The towing equipment on this truck, affectionately known as Junior's Toy, is an N.R.C. 9035 with a 35 ton underreach. It has two 30,000 lb. winches with 200' of 5/8" cable.

Clarence Cornish Wrecker Service was started in Fort Worth, Texas in 1949 by Clarence Cornish. It was purchased in 1973 by George Escott and incorporated in 1974. This Kenworth T-800 with a 400 Cummins engine has a wheelbase of 313" and a 13 speed transmission. It features air ride suspension, 4.33 rear end ratio, Jake brakes and a 60" sleeper.

The towing equipment is a Century 9055. It has a 60,000 lb. retractable boom and a capacity of 55,000 lbs. fully retracted. There are two 45,000 lb. Ramsey winches, an AM/FM radio, company 2-way radio, CB radio and a back-up camera.

Classic Towing of Maybrook, New York presents this 1995 Peterbilt Model 379 with a 425 Caterpillar engine, 13 speed transmission and 23,000 no spin rears. The towing equipment is a Century 925 SDU-Mod body. Classic serves clients with a fleet ranging from light to heavy duty tow trucks in the scenic Hudson River Valley area of New York State.

Coleman Motor Company was started in 1949. The truck shown here has a 3116 Caterpillar engine mounted on a 1991 Chevy Kodiak with a 209" wheel base. It features an Eaton/Fuller 10 speed transmission with airbrakes and a GVW of 33,000 lbs.

The towing equipment is a NOMAR/E.R. Buske model 20/25. It has a 25 ton capacity two stage boom with two 20,000 lb. winches and an MD 1030 underreach. Special features include air conditioning, a Motorola 2-way radio, Whelen strobes, bumper strobes, rear stiff legs and a C.B.

Costigan's was founded in the summer of 1987. The truck shown here is a 1994 International model 4700. It has a 180" wheelbase and a 25,000 lb. GVW. The engine is a 408 and the transmission is 7 speed. The truck is equipped with hydraulic brakes. The Jerr-Dan towing equipment is a Cougar model. It has a 12 ton boom with two 12 ton winches.

D **& G Cars'** White Knight made the journey from Kentucky to Boniface Engineering in England in January 1995 and was transformed into Dennis Harding's flagship recovery unit to suit driver John Brandon's design. This White GMC has a Cummins engine, a Fuller transmission, 296" wheelbase, 58,000 lb. GVW and airbrakes. The Boniface Recoverer towing equipment has a recovery boom that can handle 20 tons fully extended. The underreach, which has a capacity of 8 tons fully extended, is essential for buses and European-style coaches. Twin 30,000 lb. superwinch H30s provide pull.

The White Knight sports a luminescent pearl base body and two truly beautiful murals of knights riding to the rescue. General Manager Mick Jennings has 39 other vehicles at hand when trouble arises in the London area, and Keith Harding manages the company's fully equipped accident repair center.

The beautifully cared-for Mack 686SX shown here with the White Knight has EKA 2030 towing equipment with an Interstater underlift Mark 2B boom of 8 tons capacity fully extended. Its 30,000 lb. winch and 8,000 lb. winch are both Ramseys. GVW for this truck is 85,000 lbs. and the wheelbase is 230". It has a Maxidyne engine, Mack transmission and airbrakes.

Dave's Towing Service Inc. was started in 1981 by the owner Dave Barton. Besides the truck shown here, their fleet contains two other 3 axle trucks, a Landoll trailer and air recovery system. This truck is a 1979 International Conventional with a Cummins Big Cam 400 engine, Fuller 13 speed transmission and airbrakes. The wheelbase is 295" and the GVW is 55,000 lbs. The Vulcan 940 towing equipment has 90,000 lbs. capacity with one 60,000 lb. winch and another 30,000 lb. winch. The truck also features 2-way Nextel, cellular phone and sleeper.

Ce 1992 Renault C260.26 6 x 4, 300W Turbo, empattement 4,900 + 1,350 - PTAC 26,000 kgs. a été équipé par CEV avec 2 treuils force 20 tonnes, montés sur jambes de force orientables "SIDEWINDER" permettant le treuillage latéral, 2 tetes de grues orientables et ouvrantes assurant treuillage vers l'arrière. Bras de remorquage Interstater MK III à système correcteur d'assiette par oscillation hydraulique du bras, avec amortisseur de chocs atténuant les accoups dus aux freinages et aux accélérations lors des remorquages. Capacité bras rentré 21,000 kgs, en extension complète, 8,000 kgs.

The 1992 Renault C260 6 x 4 300W Turbo 4,000 + 1,350 - PTAC 26,000 kgs. shown here has been equipped by CEV with two Boniface Sidewinder side rotating stiff legs with twenty tonne winches and a MKIII fully hydraulic shock-absorbing underlift, extended rating 8,000 kgs., retracted rating 21,000 kgs.

La société **DEPANN 2000** a été crée en 1979 par M. Philippe ALLICHE et Jean-Jacques JULIEN. Six ans après une troisième personne, Bruno CHASTANG est venue renforcé l'équipe. Situé à Paris, avec quatre situations géographique, NORD, NORD EST, SUD et OUEST, DEPANN 2000 possède soixante-dix véhicules et réalise 80,000 interventions par an. Par ses résultats cette société est maintenant la première en France et parmi les meilleurs en Europe.

In Paris, France, the company known as Depann 2000 operates from four locations encircling one of Europe's largest and most prosperous cities. Dispatching from a central office, Depann 2000 trucks respond to over 80,000 calls per year with a diversified fleet of seventy-odd vehicles. Created in 1979 by Phillipe Alliche and Jean-Jacques Julien and joined six years later by Bruno Chastang, Depann 2000 has assembled a strong team of personnel and equipment. This combination has enabled Depann 2000 to become the premier company in France and to join the small group of Europe's top operators.

The 1989 Volvo N12 380W Turbo featured here with one of the world's most famous landmarks, the Eiffel Tower, has a GTW of 150 metric tons and a Jigé Lohr Mega tow package with a 25 ton and 15 ton winch.

La société Medici Dépannage fait autorité sur le secteur nord ouest de Paris, grace à une flotte de 20 véhicules parfaitement adaptés à tout type de mission du porteur VL rapide à la grue de manutention de fort tonnage. L'orgueil de la flotte est un Renault AE 500 Magnum 6 x 4 empattement 55 500HP toutes options. Equipment Jigé Lohr Mega 21, treuil principal Sepson 30T, secondaire DP 20T. Capacité de levage 21T. Télécommande radio toutes fonctions, camera de recul, carrosserie de luxe.

Medici Recovery, owned and operated by Rolland Medici, covers the northwest sector of the Paris highway system with a fleet of 20 specially adapted and outfitted tow trucks and cranes capable of handling everything from a motorcycle to the heaviest loaded trucks. The pride of the fleet is shown here, a Renault AE 500 Magnum 6 x 4 55 500 HP full options package. The towing equipment is a Jigé Lohr Mega 21 with a Sepson 30 ton main winch and a DP 20 ton secondary winch. Lifting capacity is 21 tons. This unit is also equipped with 2-way radio, back-up camera and deluxe interior package.

DeWalt Manufacturing of Channelview, Texas has been known throughout Texas and the United States since 1984 as a high quality manufacturer of a limited number of mostly heavy duty towing units. Acquired in mid-1995 by Jerr-Dan Corporation, DeWalt Manufacturing's expansion is expected by industry sources to be a substantial benefit to operators interested in top quality heavy duty tow trucks in the U.S. and abroad. This 1995 Peterbilt 379 has a 430 Detroit engine and a 300" wheelbase. The transmission is a New World Allison automatic. Outfitted to the exacting requirements of the City of Houston, this truck has an overall GVW of 64,000 lbs.

The towing equipment is manufactured by DeWalt and is an LG50 50 ton unit with 80,000 lbs. capacity and two 45,000 lb. DP planetary winches. Additional equipment includes a 3 kilowatt generator and two 500 watt Halogen lights.

Douglas Karlsson A.B., known as "A Towing" in Sweden, was started in Skövde by Hakan Karlsson and his brother Jonne in 1976 with a used DAF 300 outfitted with a Holmes 440. Today they present their CR 19 sleeper-equipped Scania R142M 6 x 2 with a V-8 DS 14 litre engine, GR 870 10 speed transmission, airbrakes, and a GVW of 24,500 tons on a 4.6 meter wheelbase. The towing equipment is by Komplet, model EKA 2030 X boom with a 20 ton capacity, 3 main winches, 30, 20 and 7 tons (front winch). The 1517 Ford Cargo has a V-8 Cummins engine, 6 speed transmission, 5 meter wheelbase, 17 ton GVW and air/oil brakes, towing equipment also by Komplet, model Peli 3500, capacity 10 tons with two main 15 ton winches and one 4 ton winch. The second flatbed has a 10 ton boom, 15 ton winch and 4 ton removable winch which can quickly be dismounted and used as a front winch.

Photo by Joachim Crus

As this photograph of their fleet shows, **Drake Towing Ltd.** is a large and diversified company serving one of North America's fastest growing metropolitan centers: Vancouver, British Columbia. Famous for their covered carriers which transport valuable vehicles locally and long distance, Drake also handles medium and heavy duty towing, as their Century 925 pictured here illustrates. They'd like to give a special salute here to the dedicated staff and drivers of Drake Towing Ltd., who daily make possible the excellent service they strive to deliver their many Canadian and U.S. customers. And they cordially invite you to call on them whenever you visit beautiful British Columbia.

Driscoll's Towing has been a mainstay in Florida for nearly forty years. These two great trucks have assisted in many a rescue on the east coast of Florida and throughout the state. The truck on the right is a 1992 International 4700 with a GVW of 29,900 lbs. and a 152" wheelbase. The DT360 engine features a 7 speed transmission. The towing equipment on this vehicle is a 12 ton NOMAR with 2 winches, each with 300' of cable.

The second truck is a 1994 Ford Super Duty with a 7.3 L turbo diesel engine and a 162" wheelbase. It has a 5 speed transmission and a GVW of 15,000 lbs. The towing equipment is a Jerr-Dan HPL with a 10 ton capacity and 2 winches. Both trucks feature rescue and recovery equipment, 2-way radio, scanner and strobe lights.

DuBois Towing of Anaheim, California is known throughout Southern California for their expert service and friendly personnel. This 1995 International 4700 Lo Pro turbo diesel has an 8 cylinder, 5 speed engine with a GVW of 18,280 lbs. It features cruise control, AM/FM stereo radio, power windows, suspension seat and stainless steel wheel covers. The towing equipment is 19' Jerr-Dan two car carrier with dual controls, a custom built steel bolt-on headboard, rear carrier-mounted Fire Bann special worklights, five custom built and painted tool boxes and a Motorola 2-way radio.

The family business is headed by Dick and Fay Boggs and anchored by the competent help of daughter Sara and son Travis.

Eagle Automotive was started in 1984 by Bob Newell and serves the Parsippany, New Jersey area. Bob currently has 9 Century wreckers, 4 Peterbilts and 2 Landoll trailers. The bigger truck is a Peterbilt 1990 375 with a 300 Caterpillar engine and a 13 speed transmission. The towing equipment is a Century 925 SDU with a 25 ton hydraulic boom. The smaller truck is a Peterbilt 1995 330 with a 3116 250 Caterpillar engine and a 9 speed transmission. It has a GVW of 33,000 lbs. The Century underlift towing equipment has a 25 ton hydraulic boom. Both of the trucks shown here feature A/C, AM/FM stereo cassette, cellular phone and 2-way radios.

Excalibur Towing, one of South Florida's premier towing operations, is owned by Ray and Maria Crego. Founded in 1983, Excalibur has grown to a fleet of 14 units, towing everything from cars to airplanes. Known as The Knights In Shining Armor, Excalibur established a reputation for courteous and prompt service. The unit is a 1995 Peterbilt 377 with a 4.25 Caterpillar engine, 913 Fuller transmission, and airbrakes. The GVW is 56,000 lbs., the wheelbase is a 256" cab to axle length, and the special American Classic Interior package rides on air ride suspension. The working end is a Century custom made 1040 with a 40 ton boom, SDU wheelift and two 45,000 lb. air operated DP winches. A 2-way radio, CB, sleeper, all fork and L-bar attachments and a mini-5th wheel attachment complete this magnificent truck.

Exclusive Towing was started in Riverside, California in 1991. This 1994 GMC has a 6.5 turbo engine that rides on a 228" wheelbase. The 5 speed transmission powers 15,000 lbs. of truck. The towing equipment is a Danco 18 with stinger. It has a 10,000 lb. capacity and 8,000 lb. winches. It features a crew cab and a Kenwood 2-way radio.

Falzone's Towing is celebrating their Golden Anniversary Year in 1995. Operated today by brothers Richard and Paul, Falzone's gives the same excellent service as their father, founder Sam Falzone, established when he started out serving the Wyoming Valley of Pennsylvania in 1945. This beautiful truck's home base is Kingston, Pennsylvania. It is a 1986 Kenworth model T-600 on a 310" wheelbase. It has a Cummins 400 engine with a 9 speed transmission and airbrakes. Overall GVW is 50,000 lbs. The towing equipment is a Century 5030/T with a 35 ton boom and 30,000 lb. winches. It features a 2-way radio, telephone and television.

43

Dewey & Mary Ann Farrington are the owners of Farrington Truck Towing & Recovery and have been doing business in Oklahoma City since 1971. They have a fleet of 9 heavy duty recovery trucks including this 1979 International with a Big Cam III 300 Cummins engine and a 13 speed transmission. The towing equipment was designed and custom built by Trebron Mfg. The boom has a 50 ton rating and extends up to 31'. It has two 45,000 lb. 2 speed planetary winches plus a 20,000 lb. deck winch with 1000' of 3/8" cable for light recovery. The Air Cushion equipment comes from several major manufacturers. Truck recovery cushions are commonplace today, but Farrington's assortment of specialty cushions for aircraft recovery, not all of which are shown here, is the largest in the U.S. Some cushions are 14' tall while others can be stacked on top of each other and have special attachments enabling them to be laced together for more lifting height.

In 1995 Eric Hammond of Fillongley Garage celebrates 35 years in the recovery industry. This company recovers everything from a motorcycle to the largest goods vehicle including heavy winching jobs, the largest to date being a 280 ton bridge. They operate from a village garage just outside Coventry, and carry out recovery for most of the main vehicle agents in Coventry as well as the bigger haulage companies in the Midland Motorway Network area. Serving also the Warwickshire and West Midland Police forces, Fillongley Garage also operates for the better motor clubs. A true family operation, Eric's son Phillip, wife and mother all work in the business, along with five other mechanics. Joining Fillongley's nine other units is this ERF 6 x 4 Model E14 powered by a Cummins 350 engine, Fuller transmission and with a GVW of 75 tons. The Brimec (Dyson) CL500L has a 21 ton tilt stinger, a 10 ton top boom and two 30,000 winches. Fillongley Garage's Managing Director is Eric Hammond, who, along with their staff, invites you to visit when in the Midlands of England.

Fox Towing has been in business in Fairfield, Ohio since 1954. It's no wonder they've been around that long when you see their trucks and talk to their customers. Fox simply delivers great service. The truck on the left is a 1995 Ford F350 with a Vulcan 804 wheelift. It has a 7.3 diesel turbo engine and a 5 speed transmission. The truck on the right is a 9370 International with a 350 Cummins engine and a 10 speed transmission. The wheel base is 270" with a GVW of 80,000 lbs. The towing equipment is a Vulcan 2020, custom installed by American Enterprises. It is the first tandem model 2020 manufactured by Vulcan. It has an integrated recovery boom and wheelift at 25,000 lbs. Both trucks have deluxe interiors, A/C, AM/FM stereo cassette and 2-way radios.

Fred's Automotive has been serving Rockland County, New York for 25 years. Located to the north of New York City, Fred's is a NY State Thruway authorized garage. This 1995 Peterbilt 379 is one of twelve trucks at Fred's. It has a series 60 Detroit engine with 430 HP that sits on a 260" wheelbase with a Fuller 15 speed transmission. The towing equipment on this truck is a Century 5030/T. The boom has a 30 ton capacity and two 25,000 lb. winches.

Garner's Family Enterprises, Inc. was started in 1980 in Fortville, Indiana. The truck shown here is a Kenworth model T-600 with a 3406 B Caterpillar engine. The wheelbase is 316" and the transmission is an Eaton-Fuller 13 speed. The truck has a GVW of 50,000 lbs., airbrakes and an eight bag air ride suspension. The towing equipment is a Century 9055/T featuring a 45 ton boom with 90,000 lbs. capacity, a 55,000 lb. wheelift and a 45,000 lb. winch. Special amenities include a 60" walk-in sleeper, 2 beds, a TV, VCR, mobile phone and refrigerator. Usually driven by Jamey Garner and the pride of the family fleet of beautiful equipment, this truck serves the trucking industry in the areas around Indianapolis, Indiana.

Gate City Towing Service, Inc. was started almost forty years ago and serves the area of Greensboro, North Carolina. This truck is a 1994 Peterbilt 377 series with a 425 HP Caterpillar engine and a Fuller RTO 14715 transmission. It has airbrakes and a 46,000 lb. Chalmers suspension. The GVW is 80,000 lbs. and the wheelbase is 298" with a 408" overall length; the truck is a tri-axle. The Century 1060S SDU towing equipment is a 360° hydraulic rotator boom with two 45,000 lb. DP planetary winches. The truck also features a cellular phone, 2-way radio and CB.

Great America Towing is located in San Jose, California. Added recently to their large and diversified fleet which operates out of five locations in this rapidly growing part of the state is this Peterbilt model 377 with a 400 Cummins engine, 13 speed transmission, airbrakes, a 300" wheelbase and a GVW of 66,000 lbs. The working end is a Century 40 ton rotator with two 45,000 lb. DP winches. The truck has been named "Strictly Business" by its owner Dino Tomassi.

Harvey's started in 1983 with a single vehicle converted for recovery by Harvey Wasson himself. With the able assistance of his wife Madeleine and their progress through difficult times to today's family operation, Harvey's operates 7 recovery vehicles and 3 service vans, carrying out work for the major auto associations and main commercial vehicle distributors in the Midlands. Recovery jobs are handled in all parts of the UK and mainland Europe. Ably assisted by Cowas, Gary, Kevin and Pete, Harvey and Madeleine maintain personal contact with all their customers, and everyone is willing to turn out 24 hours a day, 365 days a year. It's hard work but as Madeleine says, "we're all dedicated to this life!" This Scania R142H has a Scania V8 420 BHP engine, Scania 9 speed transmission, a 230" wheelbase, full air spring brakes, left hand drive, and an overall GVW of 80 tons. The Roger Dyson Recovery Systems CL 500H 4080 Enforcer has double extending hydraulic underlift and recovery boom with a 15,750 kilo capacity, two rear mounted 15,000 kg winches and a front mounted 8,000 kg winch. This beautiful unit is also fitted with a 2-way radio, rear observation camera, mobile phone, sleeper and air bag recovery equipment.

Hendrickson Towing is one of New York State's best known and most diversified towing operations. Started in 1982 by Tommy Probst and serving Long Island, the corporate umbrella also includes a fleet service division and a large body shop.   Hendrickson's is known for an emphasis on training and highly professional, motivated drivers. Called "The Most Modern Tow Truck In America" when it was spec'd out, this Mack CH613 with a Mack 350 engine has a 280" wheelbase and an 8 speed Fuller transmission. Overall GVW is 35,000 lbs. The towing equipment is a Century 5030/T with a 30 ton boom and a 30 ton capacity and was mounted to exacting standards at Michael Bigg's in Vails Gate, New York.

Hugh's Body Shop & Truck Service in Troutville, VA serves a wide variety of customers traveling along one of America's most beautiful and heavily traveled arteries: Interstate 81. Operated by Hugh and Betty Simmons and their sons Steve and Danny with a third generation in training, they own 16 trucks. This truck is a 1990 Freightliner with a conventional cab. It has a Caterpillar diesel 400 HP engine on a 364" wheelbase. The transmission is an RTO 14613 with a GVW of 80,000 lbs. and airbrakes. This truck has a front rear air lift axle and air ride suspension. The Challenger Rotator 8808 towing equipment has a 50 ton boom with a 90,000 lb. capacity and 50,000 lb. winch. This truck features a 2-way radio, telephone, 240 watt generator system, torches, jacks, all heavy duty chains and straps and a special light kit.

Interstate Chaparral Towing, run by Junior and Debbie Vandervort, provides towing and recovery services to the busy city of Austin, Texas. The twin 1994 Peterbilt 379s shown here have Cummins N14 500 HP engines with Jake brakes and 18 speed transmissions. They have 6 wheel winching brakes and 340" wheelbases. The towing equipment on these trucks are Century 9055/Ts with hydraulic extendable booms of 90,000 lbs. capacity. The twin winches on each truck both have 45,000 lbs. capacity. The trucks' useful and comfortable special features include 12 function remote controls, remote tow lights, cellular phones, 63" Unibilt sleepers, tilt & telescopic steering columns, cruise control, refrigerators, CBs, company radios and AM/FM stereo cassettes.

J **& K Recovery** of Leighton Buzzard in Bedfordshire, England presents this grouping of recovery vehicles from its larger fleet of 47 pieces diversified equipment. Owned and operated by Kevin McFadden, J & K has established a high standard of modern, strikingly well-maintained and effective equipment which serves the needs of its many clients in the south central section of the country. J & K Recovery, Ltd. handles everything from heavy haulage to motor vehicles of all shapes.

Jack's Towing of Abbotsford, British Columbia was originally started in 1955 and was owned by several people until Bill and Claudia Shuttleworth purchased the company in 1981. It consisted of 1 Ford 3 ton, 1 Ford 8000 and 3 one tons, with home built booms installed by the original owner, Jack Bushman. The fleet has expanded to 14 heavy and light duty trucks, and the company now has 23 employees. Jack's Towing does commercial, auto club, municipal and police towing and equipment handling. The Ford LTL 9000 shown here has a Caterpillar 3406B engine, a Fuller 13 speed with overdrive transmission and airbrakes. Its wheelbase is 248" and the GVW is 11,612 kilograms. The towing equipment is a Holmes 750 with a Military Deck boom of 25 ton capacity and air-controlled winches. The truck also features AM/FM stereo cassette, A/C, air ride seats, CB and 2-way radio. This truck was transporting the Friends of Towing trailer from a tow show in Saskatchewan when it stopped at a lodge in the Canadian Rocky Mountains. The picture which resulted presents the handsome truck against a truly stunning scenic background.

Photo by Claudia Shuttleworth

Jack's Wrecker Service was started in 1926. The truck shown here is a Ford F-350 XLT Series with a 351 Holley 4-barrel highout engine, 4 speed transmission, 138" wheelbase, GVW of 10,000 lbs. and power brakes. The engine is completely chromed out. The Century Formula I has power tilt, a 16,000 lb. lifting capacity telescopic boom and dual winches. This truck features an Alpine AM/FM digital cassette stereo, custom stainless steel console with 30 switches for accessories, 6 chrome plated and mounted fire extinguishers, Budnik street rod steering wheel, dual turbo stainless steel exhaust system, custom interior and a cellular phone. It also has 9 pinstriped stainless steel equipment boxes, mirrored stainless steel covered boom and stinger, chromed "L" arms and snatch blocks, stainless steel control switch for lights, Peterbilt bumper with KC fog lamps, Johnson 800 mg radio system and Billet custom made wheels. Recently added is a stainless steel turbo wing, Windjammer II series.

Jenkins Wrecker Service of Lithonia, Georgia was started in 1979 by Kenneth and Regina Jenkins. The fleet shot here with its formidable array of towing and recovery equipment is a reflection of years of late night emergency jobs, missed holidays and plain hard work. Uncompromising standards have built the company into a leader in the Atlanta area, and proud as they are of their equipment, the owners reserve their highest praise for their dedicated staff. The 1995 Peterbilt model 378 shown here has a 425 HP Caterpillar engine and a Fuller RTO 14715 15 speed transmission . It has airbrakes and a 46,000 lbs. Peterbilt suspension. The wheelbase length is 370". The unit rotates 180° for recovery or equipment setting flexibility and is a Challenger model 8808 T50 with two 45,000 lb. DP planetary winches. The truck contains a full communications package and sleeper for long distance recoveries.

Kenfield Motor Recovery's 65,000 lb. GVW recovery unit, nicknamed "Los Cojones," is constructed on the stretched chassis of a Spanish Pegaso Troner with a double drive Mercedes bogie. Boniface Engineering's Concept 3000 Olympic underlift operates in combination with two winches, a crane capable of lifting 25 tons fully extended to 6.5 meters. Kenfield is one of England's largest towing and recovery companies. Serving the busy ring road around London and many of this major city's commercial goods firms, Kenfield also provides car towing and recovery while specializing in heavy duty truck and bus recovery. Partners Colin Jeffries and Derek Firminger are active in various professional associations.

Truckee, California, a scenic little town nestled in the Sierra Nevada Mountains, is where you'll find Jim Fernhoff and Lakeside Towing. Founded in 1983, Lakeside has grown from a one truck operation to the current fleet of 25 trucks handling everything from car and truck towing to roadside truck service and in-house truck tire and mechanical repairs. This photo was taken on Old Highway 40 Donner Summit. Specializing in customer's needs, Lakeside has added 30 rental cars to its fleet to minimize breakdown inconvenience to tourists or residents of this beautiful area.

L amb & Mansfield was founded in 1978 by Thomas William Lamb, known by everyone as "Bill," in a small village in Derbyshire, England. The growing business was joined by Darrell H. Mansfield, and today from a new depot in Macclesfield, Cheshire they provide recovery service, car and commercial reservicing and accident repairs with their fleet of 24 units and their work force of 30 highly trained and dedicated men and women. Lamb & Mansfield's wide experience of all kinds of recovery jobs as well as their highly professional 24 hour service has given them an enviable reputation in the United Kingdom. This Terberg F1900 8x8 has a Volvo FIZ 400 BHP and a Volvo 16 speed transmission with a Terberg transfer box. Its wheelbase is 4,075 millimeters and its GVW is 46,000 kilograms while its GTW is 75,000 kilograms. The full airbrakes are Rockwell 8 wheel braking. The large deluxe body houses a host of auxiliary equipment including wheelifts, disc saw, chainsaw and high pressure mats to name just a few. The Boniface towing equipment has an Interstater IIE boom with 25 tonnes capacity and two Rotzler 25 tonnes/force winches equipped with 200' of 7/8" cable. The vehicle is fitted with a Bonfiglioli 40 tonne/meter lorry loading crane with 4 hydraulic extensions reaching out to 40'. The large outboard angled stiff legs are hydraulic and come complete with adjustable feet.

Lancaster's Garage has been in business since 1959 in the Concord, North Carolina area. Larry Lancaster is teaching the business to the next generation, a son and a daughter. This 1995 Kenworth T-800 has an N-14 Cummins engine and a 15 speed transmission. The towing equipment on this beautiful bright yellow and red truck is a 1995 Century 5030/T. It has a 25 ton capacity, 2-way radio and a sleeper.

Lewis Wrecker & Towing Service was started in Meridian, Mississippi in 1957. The truck shown here is an International 9370 with an NTC 400 Cummins engine. It has a 290" wheelbase, an RTO 12515 transmission and a GVW of 46,000 lbs. in the rear and 14,000 lbs. in the front. It features airbrakes with Jake brakes and 11-24-5 tires with a double frame. The towing equipment is a Challenger with a 2540 DeWalt underlift and a three stage boom. It has a 45 ton capacity and two 45 ton winches.

Lisi's Towing has been serving the area of Brewster, NY since 1971. The truck shown here is a 1988 Mack R688T with a 350 Mack engine and a 12 speed Mack transmission. The wheelbase is 240" while the GVW is 38,000 lbs., and the rear is 30,000 lbs. The Challenger 6801T-50 towing equipment is a 35 ton 3 stage boom with two 12 ton winches. The truck is also equipped with a cellular phone, 2-way radio, air conditioning, air seats and power steering.

M & W provides the area of Parsippany, New Jersey with professional recovery service. The Ford 1994 Superduty to the right has a 7.3 turbo diesel engine and a 4 speed transmission with overdrive. It has a 161" wheelbase and a GVW of 15,000 lbs. The truck features 4 wheel disc brakes, 2-way radio, police scanner, cellular phone, cruise control, A/C and AM/FM stereo cassette. The towing equipment is a Challenger 4800 with a 6,000 lb. wheellift and a capacity of 20,000 lbs. The 1978 Ford LN9000 to the left has a 230 Cummins diesel engine and a 9 speed transmission. The wheel base is 186" and the GVW is 32,000 lbs. It has airbrakes, 2-way radio, cellular phone, A/C and power steering. The Holmes 750 towing equipment is an extendable boom with a 25 ton capacity and winches of 12.5 tons capacity each.

McAllister's Recovery of Aldershot, England has chosen from its fleet this Scania 6 x 2 Model 113M with a 360 HP engine, ZF transmission and gross train weight of 65,000. It is one of the first Scanias to come equipped with a revolutionary Pioneer dump axle. The towing equipment is by Boniface Engineering, a 10 ton capacity Interstater with twin Ramsey winches. Owned and operated by Frank and Lesley McAllister, the company is a leading exponent of on-site driver safety and overall training. The special vehicle striping and personnel kit are a valuable addition to the safety of both oncoming motorists and working recovery operators at breakdown or accident sites and are specially designed by McAllister, who is also serving as the 1995-1996 Chairman of the Association of Vehicle Recovery Operators.

McCarty's Towing and Transport of Oxnard, one of California's most diversified and well known companies, presents this 1989 Peterbilt conventional Model 377 with a Cummins 400 engine, 13 speed transmission, 312" wheelbase and GVW of 50,000 lbs. The working end is a Century 1040 with a 3-stage 40 ton capacity boom and twin 40,000 lbs. capacity winches. It takes frequent long trips out of town in the service of McCarty's customers and so is comfortably equipped with a sleeper, dual air ride seats, AM-FM radio and cassette and a cellular phone.

McKinney Wrecker Service has been serving the needs of Alabamans for more than 20 years. This Peterbilt 379 has a 425 Caterpillar engine, 15 speed overdrive transmission, a 318" wheelbase and a 40,000 lb. GVW. It has airbrakes and a complete electric lockdown system. The towing equipment is a Challenger CH50. It has a hydraulic boom with a 50 ton capacity and two winches. It features a sleeper, wheelift, remote control, back-up camera and telephone dispatch.

Don and Sue Trammell of Milford Towing moved from Kentucky to the growing Cincinnati metropolitan area as young newlyweds, and opened a 76 gas station in Milford, Ohio. As part of the service station's equipment, Don added a tow truck and the rest is history. Milford Towing today operates 10 towing units ranging from the heavy duty unit pictured here to flatbeds to light duty. Son James Trammell works today in the business and after 30 years Don and Sue still work side by side at Milford. The truck shown here is a 1987 Kenworth T-600 with a 350 Caterpillar engine, a 276" wheelbase and a 13 speed transmission. It hosts a 42" sleeper. The towing equipment is a Century 5030/T with 30,000 lb. winches, a 30,000 lb. lift on the underreach and a 25 ton capacity lift on the boom.

Randy & Sue Arnett and their three sons purchased Moorman's Towing in Xenia, Ohio in August of 1990. During the first five years they have built their fleet up to consist of three one tons (a 1992 Chevrolet 3500 HD with a single line Century, a 1994 GMC 3500 HD with a twin line Century and a 1994 Chevrolet C-30 one ton with a single line Century), two car carriers (a 1992 Chevrolet 3500 HD with a 19' Challenger bed and a 1995 Chevrolet 3500 HD with a 19' Challenger bed), a 1987 Chevrolet S-10 service truck, a 1980 Freightliner with a 45 ton Challenger and a 1989 GMC Recovery Van complete with air cushions and anything else imaginable. To highlight their heavy duty recovery they have designed and built a complete line of traffic control equipment including a lighted arrow board which helps traffic flow and relieves the local law enforcement. To complement their fleet, they purchased a 4400 square foot building which they completely remodeled and which offers a warm welcome to their customers.

Photo by Lionel Mahaut

Jean Michel et Joëlle NADLER assure une sérvice dépannage jour et nuit sur un secteur autoroutier entre METZ et NANCY et une assistance MERCEDES sur un rayon de 150 kms. Le fleuron de la flotte est un MERCEDES 4044 - 8 x 4 - 440 h.p. - 40 T PTC, empattement 5m40, essieux renforcés, équipé par Jigé Lohr avec le nouveau MEGA 31, force 35 T avec un treuil SEPSON 35 T, un treuil auxiliare DP 25 T, un pare choc de poussée avec un treuil DP 10 T encastré. Toutes les fonctions hydrauliques proportionnelles sont commandées par la radio. Une caméra de recul facilite le positionnement et 5 enrouleurs automatiques pour l'air et les lignes électriques de remorquage complètent cette puissante et splendide dépanneuse.

Jean Michel and Joëlle Nadler offer 24 hour towing and recovery service along the busy super highway linking Metz, France with Nancy. In addition, Garage Nadler is an official Mercedes Assistance Service for the 150 surrounding kilometers. Their team is composed of eight employees and six trucks of which the showpiece is the truck featured here, a Mercedes 4044 40T 440 HP 8 x 4 - W.B. 54, reinforced axle. It is equipped by Jigé Lohr with the new powerful Mega 31 35T plus main Sepson 25T auxiliary winch, and a push bumper with 10T winch. Controls are all proportional hydraulic radio remote controlled. A back-up video camera and 5 automatically recoiling hoses for compressed air and electricity complete this powerful and beautiful unit's specifications.

Negoshian Enterprises serves the busy area of Newton, Massachusetts, which is to say it serves the entire area of Boston. This 1995 Freightliner FL120 Classic has a 3406C engine with 425 HP on a 289" wheelbase. It has a 15 speed transmission. The towing equipment is DeWalt LG50 with a 50 ton upper boom and a 40 ton lower boom. It has 45,000 lb. planetary winches. The unit has joy stick controls with microprocessing for gentle control. Special thanks to Don Walters.

New York Recovery was started five years ago and is located in White Plains, New York. The black truck is a 1986 Ford F 8000 with a 3208 Caterpillar engine, airbrakes and a 10 speed Roadranger transmission. It has a 25,000 lb. GVW and a 201" wheelbase. The Bro 810 Super towing equipment has a 20 ton boom, military 2 speed winches and underlift. The truck features 2-way radio and remote control hydraulics.

The red truck is a 1993 Peterbilt 378 Tandem with a 425 Caterpillar engine, airbrakes and a 13 speed Roadranger transmission. It has a 44,500 lb. GVW and a 313" wheelbase. The towing equipment is a Challenger CH 30 with a 30 ton boom that has military winches and underlift. It also features a sleeper, CB, 2-way radio, inside controls, remote control hydraulics and tinted windows.

Nowell's Towing was established in 1968 and serves the community of Woodbridge, Virginia. They perform towing, recovery and service along Route 1 and a busy stretch of the East Coast artery of I-95. The truck shown here is part of their 12 unit fleet. This completely restored 1979 Mack R700 is powered by a 676 300 Mack engine, 6 speed transmission and has a 4:1 ratio 23,000 lb. rear end. The truck has a GVW of 34,000 lbs. and a 252" wheelbase. On the working end is a 1989 NRC model 2000 20/25 with a 25 ton boom and two 10 ton winches with remote controlled axle lift rated at 7 tons fully extended to 108".

This beautiful, bright 1993 Peterbilt 377 is the pride and joy of Official Towing in St. Clair Shores, Michigan. With Ken Dombrow, a veteran Official employee since 1985 at the helm, it has serviced many a vehicle in the metro Detroit area. It features a 350 Cummins engine and a Fuller 9 speed transmission. The 227" wheelbase has a GVW of 50,000 lbs. It also features a 36" sleeper and air brakes. The 1993 Landoll Hauloll 317 has a 77,000 lb. capacity and 20 ton winches.

In 1979, Paddack's Wrecker Service began operating in Westfield, Indiana. As their excellent service became known in the area the business grew larger. Today, Paddack's operates out of Westfield and Carmel, Indiana. This photo is a testament to how well Paddack's serves the region. The HD wrecker is a 1989 Peterbilt Model 377 (Glider Kit) with a 400 Cummins engine, 300" wheelbase, 80,000 lb. GVW, 40,000 lb. Eaton rears and an RTO 11509 transmission. The three medium-duty Kodiaks in this photo each have 200 HP Caterpillar diesel engines and 6 speed transmissions. The wheelbases range from 85" to 123". Also shown here is a 1989 C70 wrecker with an 85" wheelbase and a 366 GAS with a five over two transmission. The towing equipment on these trucks are Vulcan 6000 lb. wheelifts. The rollback is a 19.5' Century with an independent wheelift. All the trucks are equipped with 800 Mhz radios and cellular phones.

Palace Garage was started in 1925 and has owned and operated this Ford tow truck since 1928 when the unit originally went to work for AAA in San Leandro, California. It has a 4 cylinder engine, 4 speed transmission, a GVW of 1.5 tons, mechanical brakes, and is outfitted with a Weaver hand crank winch with a capacity of 2 tons. Owner William Hemenez has lovingly maintained this inherited classic and often exhibits it at local parades and events. The rest of the fleet is as modern and striking as this truck is antique and beautiful.

Patriot Towing was started in 1980 and serves the Riverside, California area. This GMC Top Kick truck has a 3116 Caterpillar engine, 229" wheelbase, 10 speed transmission and a GVW of 26,000 lbs. It has airbrakes and a custom built crew cab. The towing equipment is a Vulcan with a 16 ton boom and 32,000 lbs. capacity. It has two 16,000 lb. winches. The truck also features a custom built Vulcan wheelift with 92" reach and a cellular radio. Patriot Towing is managed by Scott Troxell and is a division of Whitehouse Inc., which is headed by Arlan White and Shawn White. Two of the Whites' five children work for the company.

Petroff Towing Company is a family owned and operated heavy duty recovery service that has been in operation since 1948. They take pride in all 15 of their new, modern equipped recovery units with clean, personal, friendly services to their valued customers. Petroff offers professional towing services by professional people--all drivers are trained and certified along with hazmat personnel--in four Metro St. Louis locations, as well as offering long distance work. Their truck shown here is a Freightliner FLD-120 with a 400 Cummins engine that has a Jake brake. The truck has a 14613 Fuller transmission and Rockwell S-cam brakes. It has a 354" wheelbase, 64,500 lb. GVW, 9'8" spread tag axle and 16,000 lb. front axle. The Challenger 8808 towing equipment is a 360° rotator boom with a 12' added boom jib, capacity of 50 tons and 50,000 lb. DP 2-speed winches. The truck is loaded with special features: 6 Whelen strobe lights, Honda generator with 4 retractable quartz lights, television monitor backup system, Qualcomm communication system, 2-way radio, mobile phone, walk-in sleeper with TV and VCR, torches, cutting saws, Scot Pack and Recovery Straps on the unit.

Phil's Towing was started in 1976 and serves Philadelphia, Pennsylvania. The Freightliner FLD120 shown here has a 350 Cummins engine, a 13 speed Fuller transmission and air-brakes. It has a 50,000 lb. GVW and 292" wheelbase. The Vulcan 940A towing equipment has a hydraulic 45 ton boom with two winches: one 15 ton and one 30 ton. The truck also features A/C, power steering, AM/FM stereo cassette, 2-way radio, cellular phone and sleeper.

In 1983, Ronnie Mayer bought an F350 with a 17' bed from Southern Wrecker Sales and opened the R. Mayer company in Atlanta. Twelve years later, the R. Mayer fleet has grown to 14 trucks, including 3 Fords and 11 UDs. The majority of his business is from referrals from the high line car dealerships. But don't look for Ronnie's number in the phone book. So successful is the word of mouth around Atlanta that he's not listed. The units shown here are of a 1994 Ford 350 with a Century 211 and a 1994 UD with a 19' Century aluminum bed with independent wheelift mounted on a 94 UD chassis.

R. **U.D. Commercials Limited** of Cradley Health, England was born out of the directors Robert and Lesley Hunt's life-long love affair with commercial vehicles. Formed in 1983 with just two customers, the company has grown into a successful business, servicing a variety of commercial customers and two police recovery contracts. Located in the Black Country, their proximity to the Midlands Motorway Network provides many interesting and often challenging recoveries for their fleet of 14 vehicles. With a staff of 12, the company specialize in damage-free underlift recovery, mobile crane hire and air cushion recovery. The pride of their fleet is featured here, a sleeper cab equipped DAF chassis, model 3300/FTT95 with a DKX1160 6 cylinder turbo engine, Fuller Range Change transmission and drum brakes. The 6630 mm wheelbase supports a gross train weight of 150 tons. The Interstater Super 30 Underlift and Dominator 30 twin boom with a 30 ton capacity is manufactured by Boniface Engineering Ltd of Thetford, Norfolk, England. The unit's 3 winches are 15 tons each. A cellular telephone keeps this beautiful worker in touch with home base at all times.

Ramont's Tow Service is located in Modesto, California and has been operating since 1950. Their truck shown here is an International 4300 with an NTC 350 engine. The wheelbase is 300" and it has a 13 speed Fuller transmission, 56,000 lb. GVW and S-Cam brakes. The towing equipment is a Holmes 750 with SD12000 HDU, a twin boom, 50,000 lb. capacity and two 25,000 lb. winches. The truck also features 2-way shop radio, CB, stereo, custom tool boxes and light pylon.

Randy's Towing, owned and managed by Randy Houston, from the central office in Okanagan, provides total towing and recovery service to the north central part of Washington state. Due to the demand for professional service and high quality equipment in the area, Randy's recently opened a new location in Wenatchee. This photo presents only a small selection from their 12 truck fleet.

Rangeline Towing was started in 1969 and serves Boca Raton and Delray Beach. Their territory includes the two major highways of I-95 and the Florida Turnpike. This truck, known as "Blue Thunder," is a 1986 Kenworth T-600 with a 302" wheelbase, 9 speed transmission and a 50,000 lb. GVW. Its measurement from cab to axle is 180". The boom assembly is a Challenger CH30/T with powertilt and controls on both sides, plus in cab remote, rear stiff legs and air/electric free spools. The truck is loaded with special features, including custom dual light pylons with dual SVP-2064 lights, a 50 gallon pressurized water tank, generator with spotlight arrangement and custom under body tool boxes. It also has complete air and hand tools, trailer straps, snatch blocks, oxygen and acetylene tanks, 2-way radio, CB-PA system and telephone.

Nearly 40 years have passed since Harold Reed started Reed's, Inc. in Masillon, Ohio. Wouldn't these bright trucks be a sight for sore eyes for the stranded?

The truck on the right is a 1983 Freightliner FLC120647 with a 400 Cummins Big Cam engine. It has a 13 speed transmission on a 295" wheelbase. The towing equipment is a 1990 9035 NRC. The 35 ton boom has a 35 ton capacity and two 30,000 lb. winches. The truck on the left is a 1995 International 4700 with a DT 48 turbo engine. It has a 7 speed transmission on a 198" wheelbase for a GVW of 21,000 lbs. The towing equipment on this truck is a 1995 Jerr-Dan 19' Rustler Rollback. It has a 2 car capacity and one 8 ton winch. The truck front and center is a 1994 Ford F Super Duty XLT. It has a 7.3 power stroke turbo diesel engine with a 5 speed transmission. The wheelbase is 164" and the GVW is 16,000 lbs. The towing equipment is 1994 Chevron Rebel II with a 10 ton boom capacity and two 8,000 lb. winches. All the trucks feature stainless steel simulators.

Reynolds Towing Service, Inc. owned by Greg Reynolds has been serving the Champaign/Urbana area of Illinois for more than 15 years. These two trucks are part of Reynolds Towing's fleet which consists of 20 trucks. They also have a complete air-bag equipment recovery trailer. The truck in the front is a 1990 Peterbilt 377 conversion. It has a 350 Caterpillar engine and a 9 speed transmission. The towing equipment is a Century model 4024. The truck in the back is a 1993 Kenworth T-800 with a 430 Cummins engine. It has a 13 speed transmission that sits on a 311" wheelbase. The towing equipment is a Century model 5030/T. It features a 60" sleeper, television and AM/FM cassette stereo. The motto of Reynolds Towing is "Any time, Any place, Any size."

Rose Ledge Companies of Millers Falls, Massachusetts services Northern Massachusetts along I-91. Timothy and Pamela Tierney, along with with their children, Jayson, Emily, Timothy Jr. and Vannessa have run the shop since 1981. This 1989 International houses a 350 Cummins engine with Jake eight speed L.L., 18,000 lb. front axle and 46,000 lb. rears on a Hendrixson. The towing equipment has a 10' boom extension, a 45 ton primary winch with 400' of 3/4" cable and the secondary rear winch of 35,000 lbs. with 250' of 5/8" cable. The front mounted winch is 25,000 lbs. with 200' of 1/2" cable. All winches are two speed hydraulic, Zacklift Exporter 50,000 lbs. underreach and 120" reach. Additional equipment includes torches, 20 ton air jacks and two 20 ton marjacks. The custom body and crane are built by Rose Ledge's custom body shop, maker of custom bodies, wheelifts and attachments for the towing industry.

Louis Braun crée en 1960 le garage BRAUN dans la banlieue nord-est de Paris là où 14 ans plus tard devait s'implanter l'aéroport internationale Roissy Charles de Gaulle. La mise en service de l'autoroute du nord permet au garage BRAUN secondé par son fils Christian de se développer et de se spécialiser dans le "Dépannage-Remorquage" tous tonnage. En 1976, l'affaire personelle se tranforme en sociète anonyme et acquerit du matérièl de dépannage moderne sur une nouvelle implantation plus spacieuse en respectant l'évolution des règles écologiques.

Louis Braun started the Braun Garage in 1960 in the northwest suburbs of Paris where the international airport Charles de Gaulle would be sited 14 years later. With the assistance of his son Christian and the completion of the northern super highway, the company grew quickly specializing in towing and recovery. In 1976, the company incorporated and now operates from a new environmentally designed location with modern equipment. The truck pictured here is the largest tow truck in the world and was designed specially as a recovery vehicle.

S **& H Recovery Services Ltd.** of Doncaster, South Yorkshire, England present this DAF 95 Spacecab Model 95 400 6 x 2 with an 11 liter 400 HP engine equipped with a 16 speed 2F gearbox and retarder equipped brakes. Other special equipment includes an ECAS Computer Controlled Suspension and a reinforced heavy duty frame. The towing equipment is by Jigé Lohr, a Mega City 31 (capacity 31,000 kgs) with a radio controlled crane boom and side and rear stiff legs. Two 13,000 kg winches complete this powerful unit. S & H Recovery is owned and managed by James and John Sparrow and operates from two locations in the heartland of the United Kingdom's commercial highways.

In the middle of World War II, Sam's Towing started out with a 19Thirty-Something Ford with a crank boom and an International cabover wrecker. Later were added a 1941 Federal C2 rotating boom Army wrecker and a 1945 Diamond T 5-ton. Some of these vintage units are stored in a Wisconsin barn by the current owner of Sam's, Edward Hornbostel, until the day Eddie's son Eddie Jr. assisted by his brother-in-law John Youngs takes over and Senior can devote time to restoring these rough jewels. Eddie says they've worked too hard and faithfully to be scrapped. Since those days, Sam's has continually upgraded and improved their service and capabilities to today's equipment list of 2 mobile tire trucks, 3 mobile service trucks, 1 parts truck, 1 air bag recovery truck, 1 twenty one foot roll back truck, 1 medium duty tow truck, 3 six wheel heavy duty tow trucks, 4 six wheel heavy duty under reach trucks (two with extendable booms) and 2 tractors and low boy trailers for disabled buses, sweepers and other disabled equipment.

Sandy's Towing was started in the early 1950's and was purchased by Ted Durig in 1972. It services the busy area of metro Dayton, Ohio on a 24-hour basis. The truck shown here is a 1995 Peterbilt 377 with a 3406E Caterpillar engine. The 302" wheelbase supports a 13 speed Fuller RTO 15613 transmission. It has a GVW of 40,000 lbs. The towing equipment is a Century 9055/T with a 90,000 lb. boom. It has twin 45,000 lb. planetary winches and features a color TV, cellular phone, Motorola radio and CB.

Santa Fe Tow Service of Kansas City takes pride in their excellent equipment and up to date training. The heavy duty truck in front is a 1987 Peterbilt 377 with a 400 Caterpillar engine, 13 speed transmission, 48,000 lb. GVW and 315" wheelbase. Its towing equipment is a Vulcan 3030 with underreach and wheellift capabilities and two 30,000 lb. winches. The air cushion unit is used for transporting air cushions and all other equipment needed for Santa Fe's most challenging recoveries. The vehicle is a 1988 Ford E 350 with a 7.3 diesel engine, 4 large cushions, 2 starter cushions, 2 underwater cushions, external floodlights and generator. The two light duty trucks shown here are 1995 International 4700s with DT466 engines and 7 speed transmission. The towing equipment on the truck to the right is a Vulcan 894 Twin line with wheellift capability, while the truck in the back has a Vulcan aluminum flatbed.

Schlager Towing is located in Boston, Massachusetts and has been providing their area with recovery service for forty years now. The 1990 Ford model LTL 9000 shown here has a 444 Cummings engine and a 13 speed Roadranger transmission with overdrive. Its GVW is 80,000 lbs. and its wheelbase is 287". It has 10 wheel airbrakes and Vulcan 30/30 towing equipment with boom and winch capacity of 30 tons. The truck also features a 2-way radio, phone, cutting torches and a handy wheelift attachment used for recovering buses.

Schmitz Exxon was started in 1955. The truck on the right is a 1994 International with a 4700 lo-pro DT 408 engine. The transmission is a 7 speed with a GVW of 26,000 lbs. and 4 wheel disc brakes. The towing equipment on this truck is a Jerr-Dan Cougar with a 12 ton boom and two 5 ton winches. The truck on the left is a 1995 International with a 4700 lo-pro DT 408 engine. The transmission is a 7 speed Spicer with a GVW of 26,000 lbs. and 4-wheel disc brakes. The towing equipment on this truck is Jerr-Dan 19' Steel Shark with a 10,000 lb. capacity and an 8,000 lb. winch. It has power windows and an AM/FM stereo cassette. Both trucks are double framed and have 2-way radios.

Shaw's Foden 6x6 all wheel drive Recovery Unit is powered by a Rolls Royce Eagle 290L turbo charged engine, with a Fuller 9 speed RTX gearbox. The transfer box is a GKN 2 speed AGB 7000 Mk2 with GKN axles with inter-axle differential locking systems. The suspension is semi-elictic multi-leaf with 1600x20 tyres. The chassis frame is a bolt construction of 304x102x9.5 mm press section, complete with Foden S80 forward control GRP tilting cab, rubber and hydraulic spring suspension. Winch power is from a front Hudson Wharton 10 ton hydraulic, with 45m of 18mm cable. The rear mounted Rotzler with 85m of 24mm cable gives 25 ton capacity. The rotator unit has a 7.7m reach lifting capacity of 12,500 tons at 2,900mm; 7 tons at 5,300mm; and 4.8 tons at 7.7m; slewing angle of 200°, lifting capacity at 5.5m high of 14 tons, and 9.5m of 9 tons, plus a Rotzler hydraulic recovery winch with a rope diameter of 16mm. The damage-free underreach recovery boom has a capacity of 8 tons, and 4 tons at full reach. The rear anchor/stiff legs have a maximum earth anchorage of 50 tons. The bogie blocking device, operating on the rear drive axle, has a transfer value of 5 tons. The unit is also equipped with hydraulic side stabilizer jacks. It is equipped with remote controls (for the complete recovery unit or the underlift operation) plus a full set of lifting fork attachments, straps, chains and auxiliaries, which are housed in the British Army specification bodywork. Home is Markyate, England.

Shroyer's & Central Towing, Inc. operates out of the Lansing, Michigan area. They have been in business for more than 60 years! This 1970 Diamond REO C116 has a 255" wheelbase and a 13 speed Fuller transmission. The GVW is 50,000 lbs. It was built into a tow truck in 1976 by Shroyer's and ran until 1990. At that time the old towing equipment was removed, the frame was lengthened and tandems were added. It now has a boom with a 50 ton capacity that extends 10 feet and has a power up and power down. It has a 60,000 lb. push hydraulic cylinder, a hydraulic spade on the rear and three lift cables over the boom. It is cable supported and equipped with one 30 ton Garwood winch and three 20 ton Braden winches. It is completely operated by hydraulics.

Skeet's of Conover, North Carolina opened for business in 1987. Owned and operated by Stacey and Skeet Hartis, the company has experienced steady growth due to its pace-setting emphasis on professionalism and quality service. This 1994 F-450 Ford has a 7.3 Turbo diesel engine with a manual transmission, disc brakes an 84" C.A. GVW is 14,500 lbs. and the towing equipment including the 10 ton capacity boom is by AATAC which also designed the special molded-in tool boxes. Other special equipment includes a Uniden 800 Mhz 2-way radio and the special candy red and blue paint. Last but never least, the owners add "Special thanks to Dad!"

Photo by Trevor Roper

SOS Recovery is a family business operated by father, mother and sons in Bradford, West Yorkshire England. Established in 1979 and serving a wide range of commercial, private and municipal clients, they now have a fleet of 11 recovery vehicles of which the pride of the fleet is this Foden 4400. This vehicle is powered by a 400 BHP Caterpillar engine with a 13 speed Heaton gear box and has 10 ton Rockwell air suspension axles and an overall GVW of 80 tons. The towing equipment is an Interstater MK111C with twin radio remote 15 ton winches and hydraulic stiff legs.

Statewide Towing & Recovery was started by its present owner Chris Kirk ten years ago in Riverside, California to meet the growing needs of one of California's most densely populated areas. This beautiful machine is a 379 Peterbilt with a 3406 Caterpillar engine. The wheelbase stretches 323". It has a 15 speed transmission, a GVW of 58,000 lbs. and airbrakes. The towing equipment is a 50 ton DeWalt. The 50 ton boom has a 100,000 lb. capacity and 40,000 lb. DP planetary winches. The truck features a 40" sleeper, 40 channel CB, a rosewood dash, television and a microwave!

Superior Towing was started six years ago and serves the beautiful district of Riverside, California. The truck on the right is a 1993 model 379 with a 500 E Model Caterpillar engine and a 15715 transmission. The wheelbase is 328" and the GVW is 60,000 lbs. The boom is a DeWalt 50 ton. The 1995 model 379 truck on the left is slightly smaller with a 315" wheelbase. The towing equipment is DeWalt 25 ton underlifts.

Technique Towing was started in July, 1994. The truck shown here is a 1992 Freightliner with a 460 Detroit engine. It has a 9 speed transmission and a 295" wheelbase. The GVW is 80,000 lbs. and it has Jake brakes and on board scales. The towing equipment is a Miller Industries 3030. It has a 30 ton boom with a 30 ton capacity. It features a 2-way radio, sleeper and remote control on all functions. Technique Towing has 7 small trucks and 3 big rigs, plus airbags with the trailer.

Located in Southborough, Massachusetts, **Ted's of Fayville** has been serving the New England area since 1929. The owner Peter Aspesi first began working for Ted's some forty years ago, while he was a high school student. The air cushion recovery unit shown here responds to calls for assistance from Ted's customers and other towing companies throughout New England. The vehicle is an International S1900 with a Caterpillar 3208 engine, an Allison automatic transmission, airbrakes, a 33,000 lb. GVW and 236" wheelbase. It has a generator, lights, cut off saw and spill clean up material as well as other necessary equipment for recovery and air cushion jobs.

This unit is owned and operated by Transport Towing, Inc. of Joliet, Illinois which has been in business since 1976. This technology packed unit was purchased to eliminate lane blockage during Interstate Highway recoveries. The truck is a 1992 Peterbilt powered by a 425 HP Caterpillar Power Plant. The transmission is an 8 speed with a double reduction low. The 334" wheelbase truck sports air ride suspension with independent monitoring gauges. The recovery bed is a 1992 NRC Industries 45 ton sliding rotator. The boom assembly rotates 270° and the boom and base slide to the rear of the truck 10'. The truck self levels itself, walks sideways and can be operated by remote control.

Truck Tire and its sister company Overland Equipment are located in Landover, Maryland in the heart of the Washington DC Metropolitan area. Now also a full service equipment distributor, the company's fleet of vehicles can solve just about any transport related problem that might occur. Owner Jim Mills is a Maryland native, but chose to locate in the Landover area due to the growing needs of all types of transport and road traffic in the area for quality service. When trouble arises, they get there with whatever it takes to solve the problem. From a complete commercial tire inventory to all classes of towing to over the road transport and tow truck body and parts sales, Truck Tire/Overland Equipment is at your service.

In 1981 John Tumino started John's Teaneck Garage as a small gas station in New Jersey. In the next fourteen years he would go on to build one of New Jersey's finest and most professional towing companies - Tumino's Towing. Still located in Teaneck, in a beautiful stone building, Tumino's is the shop of choice for many large bus companies, dealers, police departments and private individuals. John also owns a body shop in Hackensack, New Jersey. The truck on the right is a 1990 Peterbilt 375 with a 300 Caterpillar engine, 13 speed transmission and a 43,000 lb. GVW. The towing equipment is a Challenger T-50 with a 20 ton boom and a 50,000 lb. capacity. It has a 3 stage underreach and twin Ramsey winches. The truck on the left is a 1989 Peterbilt 357 with a 3406B Caterpillar 400 HP engine. The towing equipment is a Century 1040 SDU with a 40 ton 2 stage boom and a 3 stage underreach with a 40 ton 45,000 lb. capacity. It has twin Ramsey winches with 30,000 lb. capacity. Both trucks feature 2-way radio and AM/FM cassette stereo.

Since 1955, the West Coast of Florida has been served by the Upman family, initially with a full service gas station and one tow truck but steadily evolving into the present day professional towing service in Sarasota. While Randy's father will always retain the honorary title of Chairman, Randy Upman today runs an operation of 10 trucks and 10 employees. Randy and his wife Lisa are very active in their state association, Professional Wrecker Operators of Florida, and they have built a company with high standards of professional conduct and a diversified fleet capable of handling any problem on the highways of Florida.

Wards of Burnley was started in 1975 by Graham Ward. The truck shown here is a Man 24/291 with a Man 291 engine, 13 speed transmission and full airbrakes. Its wheelbase is 216" and its GVW is 65 tons. It has a heavy duty rear bogie, also by Man.

The towing equipment is Dyson's Enforcer 15, built in 1992. Its underlift boom is hydraulic extending with a capacity of 20 tons retracted and 9.5 tons extended. The two winches are 15' Boughton hydraulics. This truck also features a mobile phone, rearview cameras, MFC high pressure mats and all types of accessories.

Watty Garage, founded in 1966, is a multi-service body shop, car wash, fuel center and towing facility serving the western coast of Belgium in the busy Ostend area. The recovery service division ranges over much of Europe and all of Belgium providing professional towing and recovery with a total of 6 units. Pictured here is "baby" of the fleet, the award-winning Toyota equipped by Jigé-Lohr and the Volvo-mounted Century rotator, only the second of its type in Europe. Robert Watty and his son Luc and their families offer service and equipment second to none and welcome visitors to their facility with warmth and sincerity. This Volvo NL 12 Intercooler has a 6 cylinder 12000cc 405 HP Volvo engine and a 12 gear transmission. From front axle to rear axle it measures 5.8 meters while its GWV is 24 tons. The brakes are Jake brakes Voith 4000Nm and it also has a rear view camera, telephone and sleeper. The towing equipment is a Century which was installed by Jigé-Lohr. The rotator boom has a 35 ton capacity and two 30,000 lb. winches. There is a 60,000 lb. winch on the back of the truck and a 30,000 lb. winch on the front bumper. The Toyota Landcruiser has a 4.2 liter 6 cylinder diesel engine and a 5 speed transmission. Its measurement from front to rear axle is 3 meters and its GVW is 3 tons. The towing equipment is a Jigé-Lohr Mid City IV with a 1.2 ton underlift. Two 3.5 ton electric superwinches are installed; one on the underlift and one on the front bumper. The truck is also equipped with a telephone.

In 1986 Ken Weber and his family started Ken Weber Truck Service doing semi-truck repairs. One year later they branched out to towing. Since then they have added three car tow trucks, three flatbed carriers and three heavy duty tow trucks, one of which is shown here. With the able assistance of his wife Mary, son Ken Jr., and daughters Tracy and Wendy, Weber runs a large shop with approximately 20 employees serving municipal and commercial accounts, as well as private accounts in the Pewaukee area and Waukesha County. Ken is also on the board of directors of the Wisconsin Towing Association. This 1991 Peterbilt 379 conventional has a 3406 Caterpillar engine with a brake saver. The wheelbase is 338 inches and it has a 15 speed double overdrive. The towing equipment is a Century 5030/T3 with a hydraulic, extendable boom with a capacity of 30 tons. This incredible machine features a 63" sleeper, 2-way radio, CB radio, AM/FM cassette, cellular phone, police scanner, TV, refrigerator, back-up camera, in-cab controls, aluminum roll-up doors, cordless tow lights, full assortment of forks and attachments, pintle hook, 5th wheel, portable generator and lighting system, cutting torches, complete impact tool set, midship hydraulic spades, deluxe aluminum package and heated hydraulic system.

Williams Heavy Duty Wrecker Service was started in January of 1982 by Johnny R. Williams. Presented here is the company's 1977 Kenworth W700, with a 3406 B 460 HP engine, 10.5 Eaton air brakes, an RTO 14613 transmission and a 277" wheelbase. Overall GVW is 58,420 lbs. This truck has an Eaton Postrac differential, front and rear 4:10 ratio, directional aluminum wheels and all Bridgestone tires. The working end of this beauty is a DeWalt LG 50 with a 50 ton boom and two DP dual speed 45,000 lb. air release winches. Completing this truck's specifications are a two-way radio, cellular phone and TV.

Wilton Service Center of Wilton, New York has been operating since 1977 on I-87 in upstate New York. The truck shown here belongs to a fleet of eight trucks. This 1977 Auto Car Constructor has a 350 Cummins engine, a 15 speed Roadranger transmission. It has 50,000 lb. rears, 18,000 lb. front axle and a 300" wheelbase. The towing equipment was manufactured by Wreckers International, and it was the last "Recoveror" ever made in 1983. The three stage hydraulic boom has a capacity of 40 tons, and is equipped with a 20 ton drag winch, full rear hydraulic stiff leg and dual hydraulic side outriggers. The body is custom made with a front tunnel-through box. There are only a few units like this left in the U.S.A.

Photo supplied by owner

Winebrenners of Elyria, Ohio has been in business since August of 1983. With the years of experience as General Manager of the company known as Elyria Auto and Truck Service, the new owner Clinton Winebrenner built on the previous company's excellent reputation and embarked on upgrading all the equipment. This light duty unit is an example of the fleet. The Vulcan tow unit has a boom rating of 8,000 extended and 20,000 retracted; the underlift's rating is 4,000 and 2,500 on tow. The chassis is a 1994 Super Duty 7.3 diesel purchased from Ed Mullinax Ford and the unit was put together by American Enterprises of Oregon, Ohio.

WreckMaster wishes to commend Jerr-Dan Corporation, the first of the major manufacturers to recognize the need of the towing and recovery industry instructors for modern training equipment. The company then stepped forward to supply the four lead WreckMaster instructors with Jerr-Dan equipment. This contribution to training excellence guarantees the student exposure to the latest in safe equipment technology and presents WreckMaster training material at its best. These units can be seen throughout North America at the WreckMaster hands-on seminars.

Woody's Wrecker Service has been in business for more than 15 years serving the greater Waco, Texas area. Their bright red trucks are easy to spot and a welcome sight to stranded motorists. The fleet is all painted the same brilliant cherry color, and typical of the trucks would be a Ford F-350 with a 460 engine on a 137" wheelbase, 4 speed overdrive transmission and a GVW of 11,000 lbs. The towing equipment on this truck is a Century 412 with a 4,000 lb. wheelift and dual winches.

A & M Automotive is a multi-faceted towing, automotive service, crane and rigging company based in High Point, North Carolina. Owner Tim Nall's dedication to service is encapsulated in the company's motto: "Don't fuss, call us." And over the years this approach has proven effective. The two young Nall children, Anamarie and Seth, appear in all the company's advertising, adding a friendly touch to the high tech nature of the company's business.

Gene's Towing was started in 1961 and serves the area of Tacoma, Washington. The family-run company now has three locations and takes pride in the fact that 75% of their business is repeat and referral work. They serve several specialized needs in the towing industry, including the field of hazardous materials. The truck to the right is a Freightliner FLD120 with a 350 Big Cam IV engine, a 293" wheelbase and a 14613 transmission. It has a GVW of 58,000 lbs. and airbrakes. The towing equipment is a Century 925 SDU with a 25 ton boom and dual 25,000 lb. Ramsey winches. The truck features Motorola 2-way radio, Bearcat, a 42" air-conditioned sleeper and air-conditioned cab. The truck to the left is an AV6 International F-2674 with a Cummins 400 Big Cam IV engine, a 293" wheelbase and a 14615 transmission. It has a GVW of 62,000 lbs. and airbrakes. The towing equipment is a Challenger 6802 with a 3 stage boom and dual 25,000 lb. Ramsey winches. The truck also features AM/FM stereo and air conditioning.

J & J Towing of Margate, Florida was started in 1984. The truck shown here is a 1994 Peterbilt model 4/25 Caterpillar. It has a 13 speed transmission and airbrakes. The towing equipment is a Century 5030/T with a 30 ton boom and a 50 ton winch. Special thanks to John Hawkins at Century for helping to build this great truck, Mike Pardon of Broward Truck for the paint layout and Harold Murphy for the paint work.

J & J Towing services the busy Maryland/Virginia/ Washington, D.C. area out of Lothian, Maryland. This vintage International RDF212 truck has a 180 Cummins engine and a 5 speed transmission with a 3 speed auxiliary. The Weld/Built Body has a 30 ton capacity, dual booms and two 60,000 lb. winches. This truck is just one of eight trucks in the J & J fleet.

Select Towing was started in 1984 by John and Reneé McElroy with one truck. At present their fleet consists of 15 units and specializes in the transport of auction vehicles, heavy duty recovery and Grade A service to motor clubs and dealers. A family run business, Select is most proud of the job longevity of their fine employees in a business normally proven to be high-turnover. Select does work for several police departments and has a high level of participation in community events as well as the T.O.W.E.D. program. This Kenworth T-800 has an N-14 370 Cummins engine and a 13 speed Roadranger transmission with overdrive. Its GVW is 52,000 lbs. and its wheelbase is 232". The towing equipment is a Challenger CH-30 with a 30 ton 2 stage boom and winches of 25,000 lbs. each.

Van Amerongen b.v. of Arnhem, Holland, was established in 1965 by Hendrick J. van Amerongen. The company's first tow truck was a Volkswagen with a dolly behind and Henk, as the founder is always called, was the only employee. In three months, he was happy to have a grand total of 12 jobs. Today, the company does 700 calls in a month and 55 people are employed. The company serves a wide variety of customers and handles everything from cars to the heaviest goods vehicles. This antique shown here is the same model as Henk's first tow truck; it's an Opel Bletz 1969, and sported a one ton crane--here a replica of the original Weaver crane. The Mercedes is a Model 2635 with a Hiab knuckle boom crane 30 metric tons capacity and a 5030/T Century lift.